SOLAR SYSTEM
ACTIVITY BOOK

POLLY CHEESEMAN
AND BETHANY LORD

ARCTURUS

CONTENTS

ARCTURUS

This edition published in 2024 by Arcturus Publishing Limited
26/27 Bickels Yard, 151–153 Bermondsey Street,
London SE1 3HA

Author: Polly Cheeseman
Consultant: Helen Giles PhD
Illustrator: Bethany Lord
Editor: Violet Peto
Designer: Rosie Bellwood-Moyler
Design Manager: Jessica Holliland
Managing Editor: Joe Harris

ISBN: 978-1-3988-3632-7
CH010504NT
Supplier 29, Date 0224, Print run 00004297

Printed in China

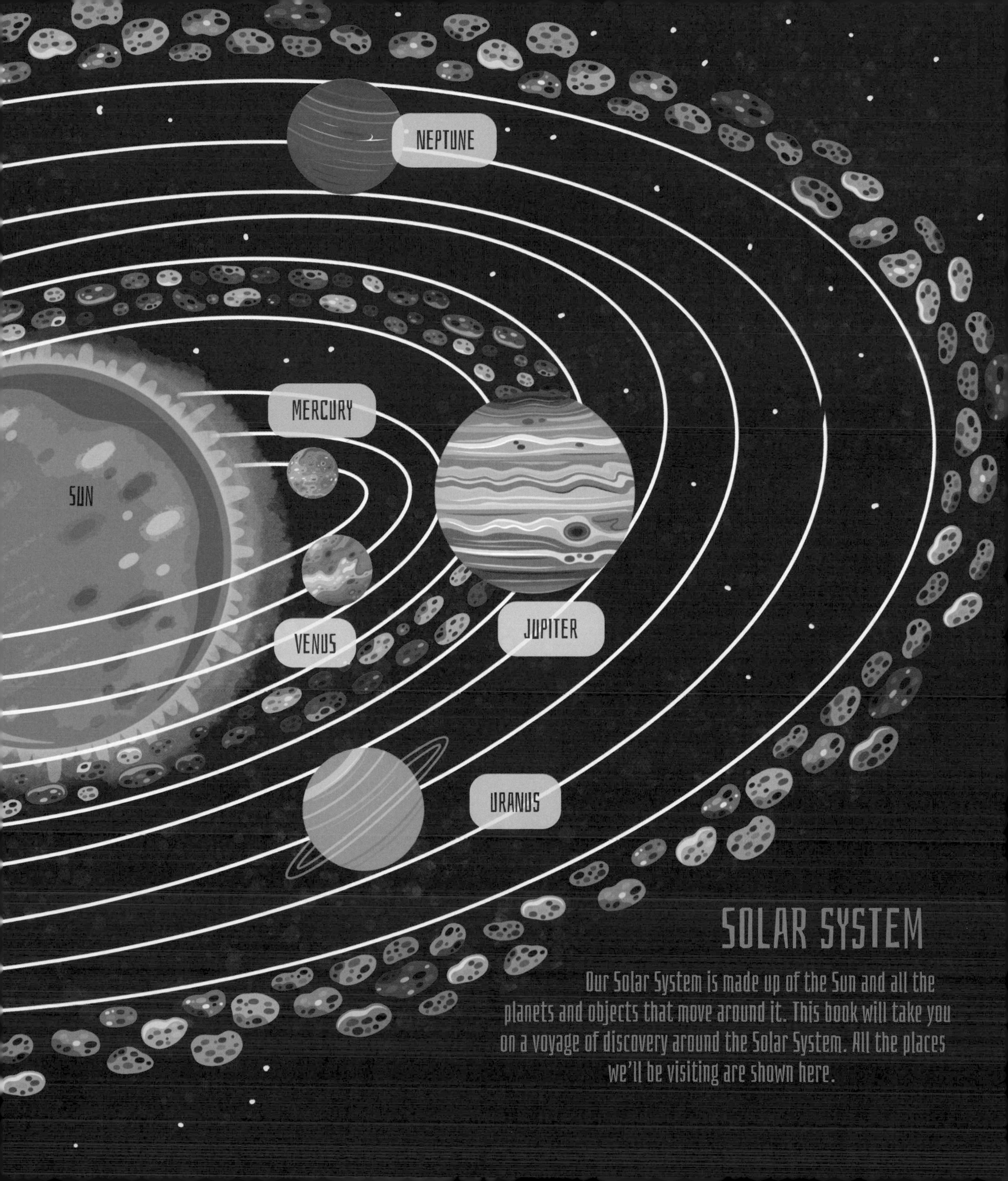

NEPTUNE

MERCURY

SUN

JUPITER

VENUS

URANUS

SOLAR SYSTEM

Our Solar System is made up of the Sun and all the
planets and objects that move around it. This book will take you
on a voyage of discovery around the Solar System. All the places
we'll be visiting are shown here.

WHAT IS THE SOLAR SYSTEM?

Our Solar System is just one of billions of planetary systems in the Universe. It is made up of the Sun and lots of different objects, including planets, dwarf planets, moons, asteroids, and comets.

• The Sun is in the middle of the Solar System. All the planets orbit, or move around, the Sun.

There are eight planets in the Solar System. Can you name them all?

Can you spot all the objects above in the picture of the Solar System?

BIRTH OF THE SOLAR SYSTEM

The Solar System we know today started to form around 4.6 billion years ago. But how did it all begin?

Match the pictures below to the correct descriptions to find out how scientists think the Solar System formed.

1

2
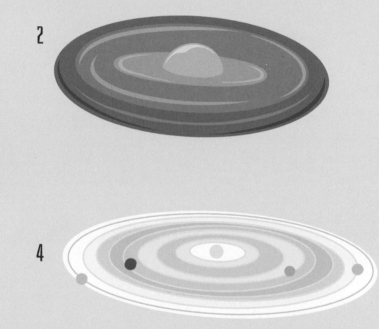

3

4

5

A. Later, part of the cloud collapsed in on itself and became a flattened spinning circle of dust and gas.

B. The Sun ate up almost all the material around it. The leftover bits clumped together into bigger and bigger chunks.

C. Material gathered in the middle, creating a huge amount of heat and energy. The Sun was formed.

D. Over millions of years, the chunks became planets and dwarf planets. Smaller leftover pieces became moons, asteroids, and comets.

E. Our Solar System started from a cloud of gas and dust, which was part of a much bigger cloud.

The Sun is so massive that its gravity pulls all the planets into orbit around it. In our solar system, smaller rocky planets formed near the Sun, and larger gassy, icy planets formed farther away.

A JERIPUT

B PETENUN

Rearrange the letters to spell out the planet names. Then number them from 1 to 8, with 1 being the closest planet to the Sun, and 8 being the farthest.

C RAMS

D ATRUNS

E HATER

F RUNUSA

G SENUV

H CURRYME

THE SUN

The Sun is our local star. Like all stars, it is a massive ball of burning gas. The Sun gives out enormous amounts of light and heat, which we call sunshine.

OUR BRIGHTEST STAR

Although there are countless other stars in the sky, for us on Earth, the Sun is the brightest by far. This is because it's much closer to us than any other star.

There are lots of different types of stars, such as white dwarfs, blue giants, and red dwarfs. Cross out the letters that appear three times or more to discover the type of star our Sun is.

BHYEBLHLOHBW   DCWTACTRFCT

▪ The Sun measures around 1.4 million km (865,000 miles) across. Even though the Sun is an average-sized star, at least a million Earth-sized planets could fit inside it.

- - - - - - - - - - - - - - - -   - - - - - - - - - - - - - - - -

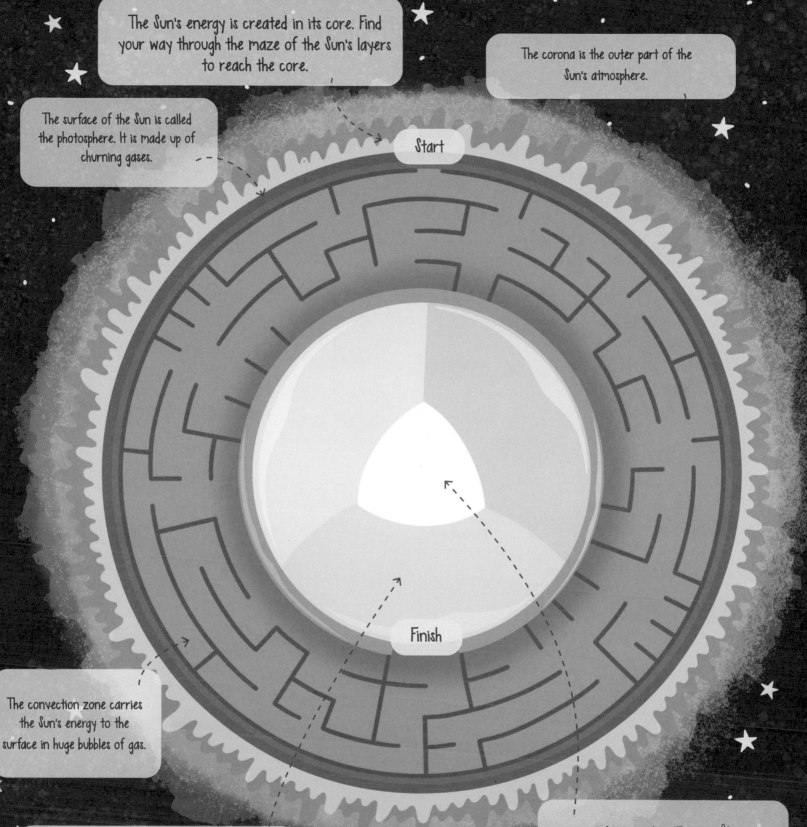

DAY AND NIGHT

All the planets spin around as they orbit the Sun. The side of a planet that faces the Sun is bathed in sunlight. The side of the planet that faces away is in darkness.

A day on Earth lasts 24 hours, because this is how long it takes to spin around once. Other planets have shorter or longer days.

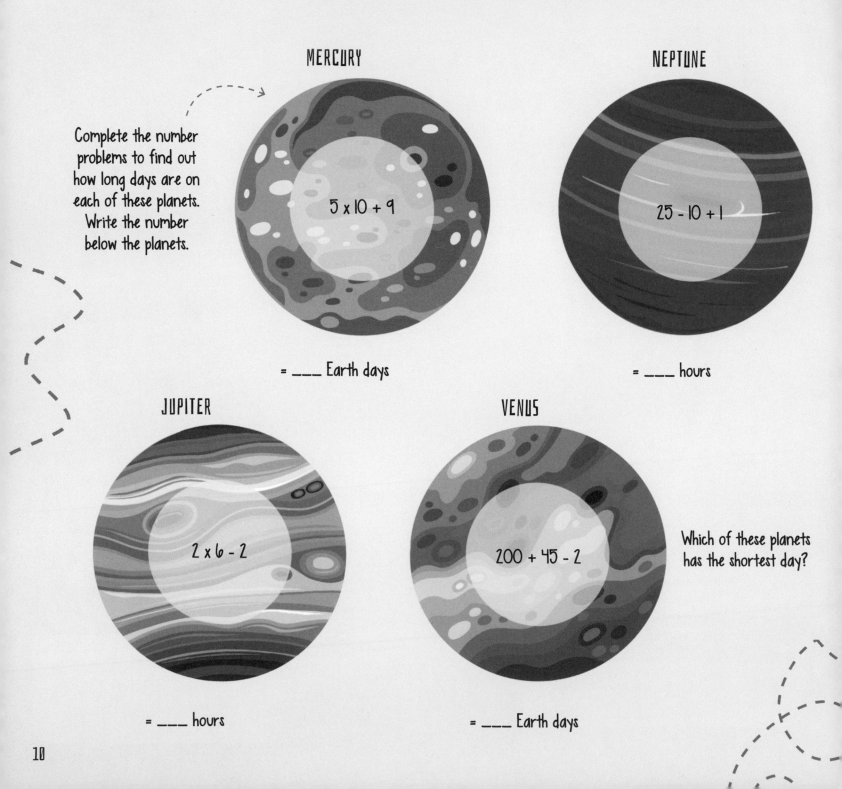

Complete the number problems to find out how long days are on each of these planets. Write the number below the planets.

MERCURY

$5 \times 10 + 9$

= ___ Earth days

NEPTUNE

$25 - 10 + 1$

= ___ hours

JUPITER

$2 \times 6 - 2$

= ___ hours

VENUS

$200 + 45 - 2$

= ___ Earth days

Which of these planets has the shortest day?

The time it takes for a planet to orbit the Sun is called a year. A year on Earth is 365.25 days.

Can you guess which planet in the Solar System has the longest year?

A. Neptune

B. Saturn

C. Venus

Can you match each of these planets to its silhouette?

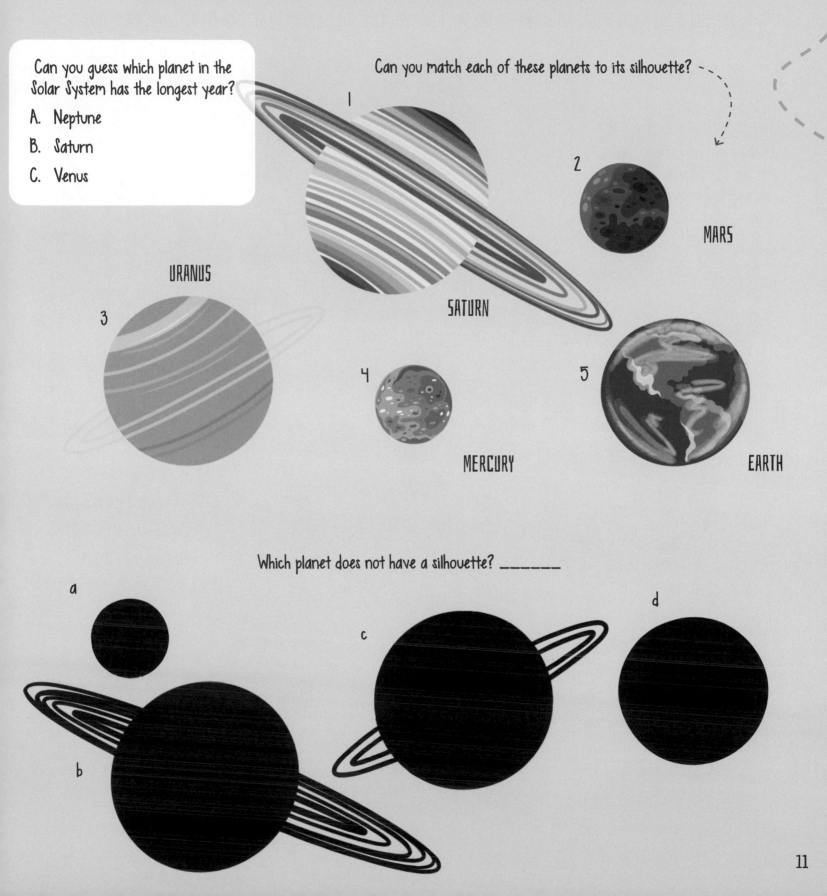

1

2

MARS

URANUS

3

SATURN

4

5

MERCURY

EARTH

Which planet does not have a silhouette? _____

a

b

c

d

11

FEATURES OF THE SUN

The Sun is not just a bright yellow ball in the sky. Close up, its stormy, explosive surface is constantly changing.

Bubbles of hot gas push up to the Sun's surface from below. How many bubbles can you count here?

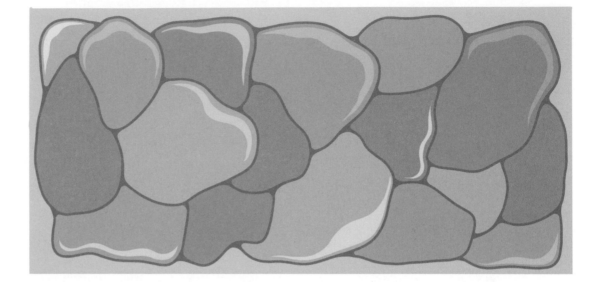

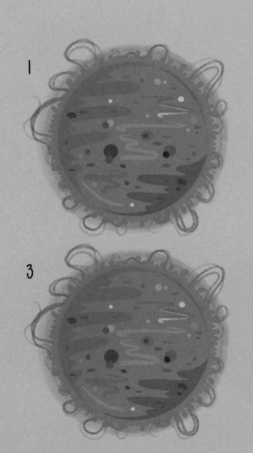

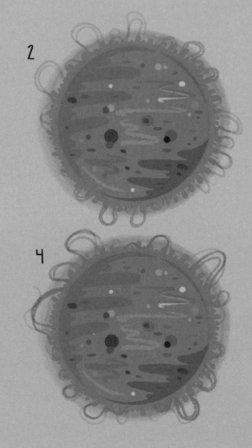

1

2

3

4

Can you spot the odd Sun out?

▪ Solar flares are sudden bursts of energy on the Sun's surface. They appear as bright flashes.

▪ Sometimes huge loops of material, called solar prominences, flow out from the Sun.

Sunspots are dark patches that appear on the Sun's surface, where the temperature is slightly cooler. Sunspots are always changing. Some appear for a few days, others last for weeks.

Can you find the coordinates of all the sunspots in the picture below? Write them in the spaces under the grid.

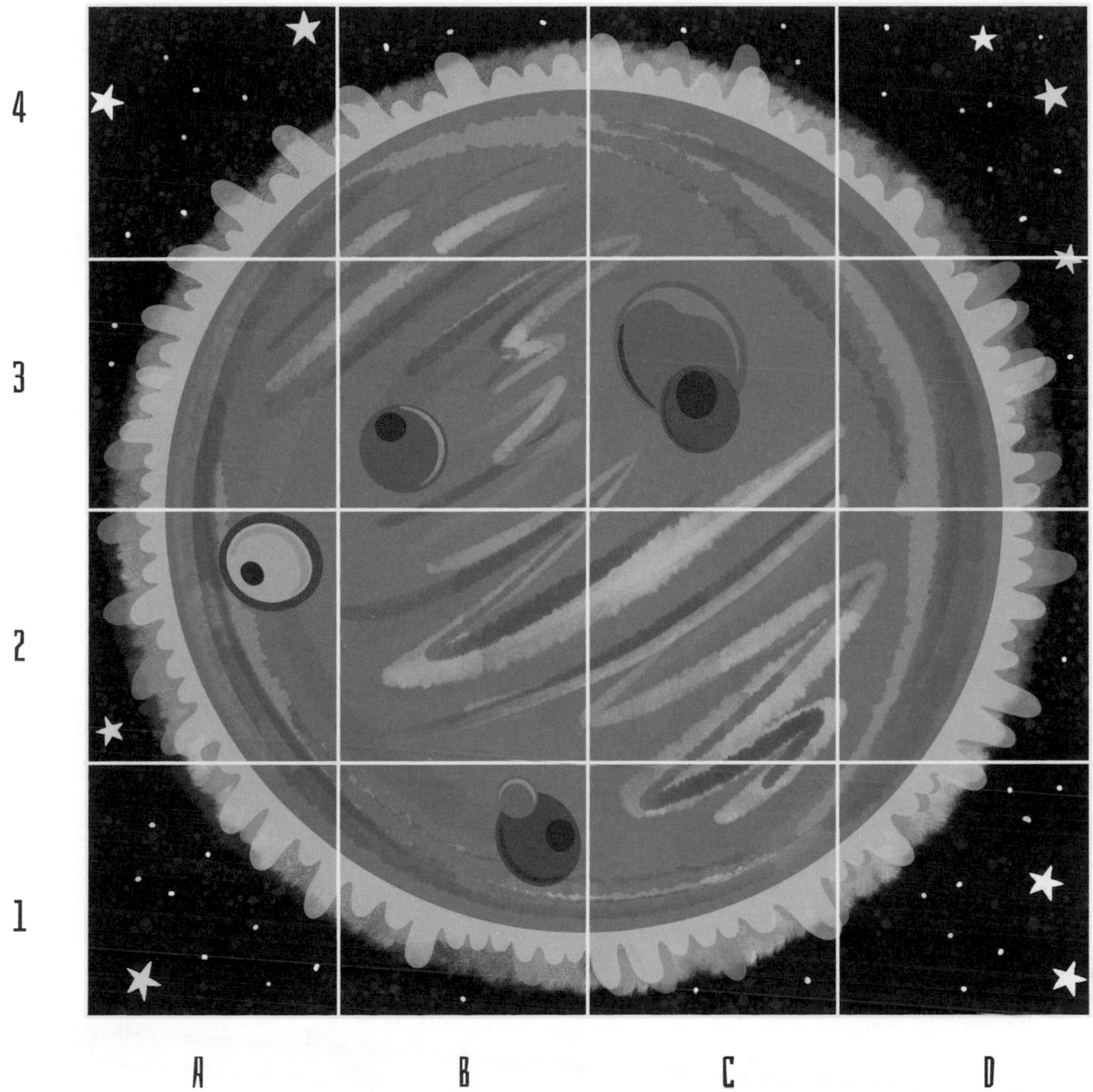

-          -

-          -

• Never look directly at the Sun. The light is so bright and powerful it could damage your eyes.

THE SOLAR WIND

The Sun sends out a constant stream of particles into space—but usually we can't see it. This is the solar wind. When the solar wind hits Earth's North and South Poles, the particles create a beautiful light display called an aurora.

The aurora borealis is an amazing sight in the sky near Earth's North Pole. Complete this jigsaw scene. Which puzzle piece does not fit?

Particles in the solar wind interact with the gases in Earth's atmosphere, creating different lights.

Follow the trails to see what effect oxygen and nitrogen creates.

1. Oxygen

2. Nitrogen

A. Blue, purple, and pink lights

B. Green lights

Earth is not the only place to see auroras. Use the code cracker below to find out two other places where auroras have been spotted.

A	B	C	D	E	F	G	H	I	J	K	L	M	N	O	P	Q	R	S	T	U	V	W	X	Y	Z
Z	Y	X	W	V	U	T	S	R	Q	P	O	N	M	L	K	J	I	H	G	F	E	D	C	B	A

HZGFIM ZMW QFKRGVI

_ _ _ _ _ _   _ _ _   _ _ _ _ _ _ _

THE INNER PLANETS

The four planets closest to the Sun are Mercury, Venus, Earth, and Mars. They are known as the rocky planets, because they have rocky surfaces, with metal and rock inside.

MERCURY

The closest planet to the Sun is Mercury. It is also the smallest planet in the Solar System. It is just slightly larger than Earth's Moon, and looks a bit like it, too.

Just like our Moon, Mercury's surface is covered with craters. Look at the craters below. Can you put them into matching pairs?

▪ Craters are huge hollows made by asteroids, meteorites, and comets falling from space and hitting the surface.

▪ Mercury does not have a moon.

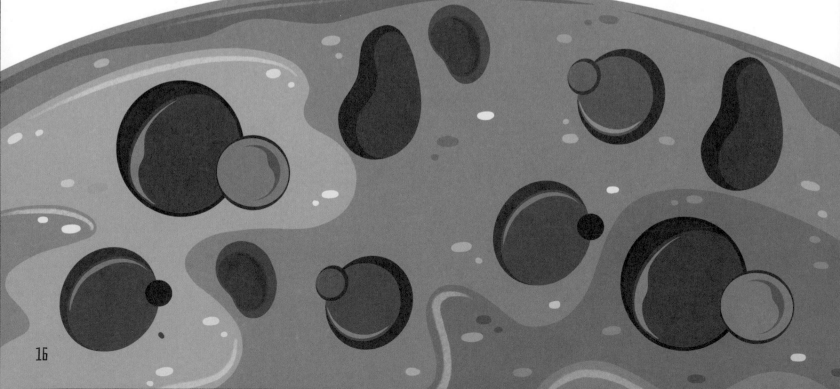

The first spacecraft to visit Mercury was Mariner 10 in the 1970s. This unmanned probe collected pictures and data as it flew by Mercury. Much of what we know about Mercury comes from the Mariner mission.

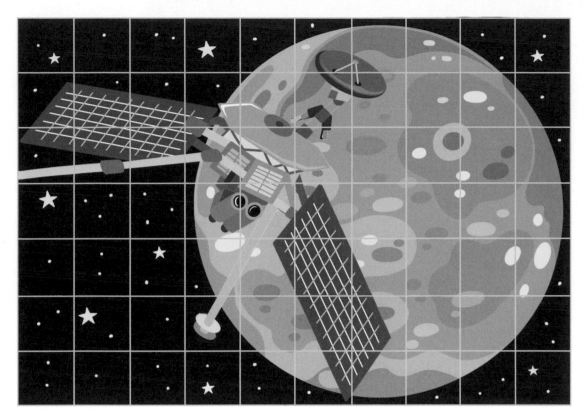

- People have known about Mercury since ancient times. When at its brightest, it can be seen with the naked eye.

- Mariner 10 discovered that the conditions on Mercury are such that no life could exist there.

Draw Mariner 10 exploring Mercury by copying the picture square by square.

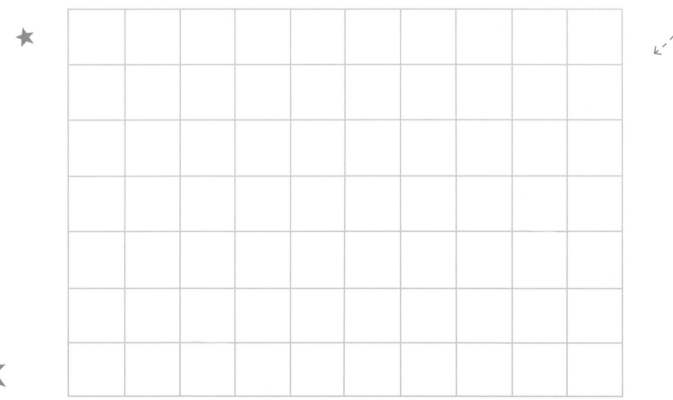

PLANET OF EXTREMES

A year on Mercury is equal to 88 Earth days, because that's the time it takes to orbit the Sun. However, because it spins so slowly, Mercury has fewer than two sunrises in each of its years.

Mercury is the closest planet to the Sun, so it gets extremely hot. Its daytime temperature can reach 427 °C (800 °F). Can you guess what Mercury's temperature is at night?

A. The same as daytime

B. 0 °C (32 °F)

C. -180 °C (-290 °F).

The surface of Mercury is rocky and dusty. Inside there is a very large metallic core. Unscramble the letters to reveal which metal the core is.

NORI

_ _ _ _

Sometimes, Mercury can be seen crossing in front of the Sun if Earth, Mercury, and the Sun are all in line. When a planet passes in front of the Sun like this, it is called a transit.

Find the coordinates listed on the right on the picture of the Sun to plot Mercury's transit. Draw a dot in each square, then join up the dots.

E5   B2   C3   D4

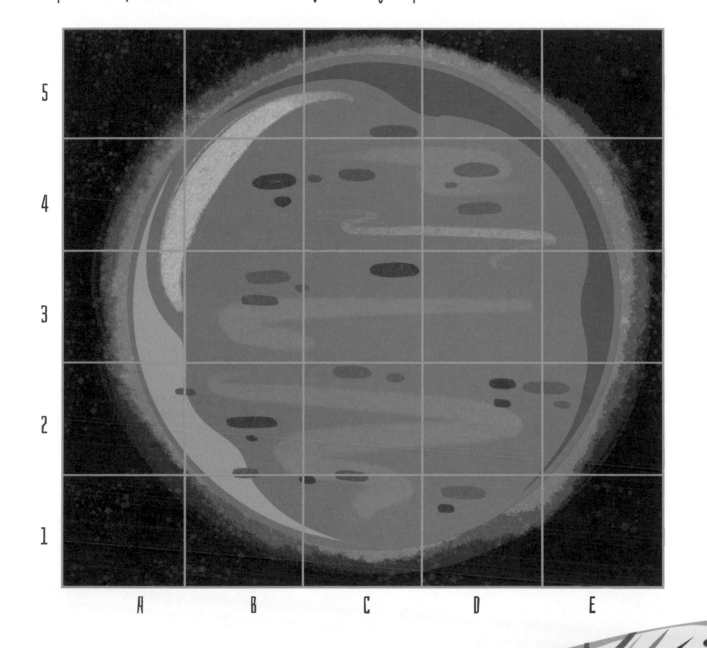

The Caloris Basin is the largest crater on Mercury. Can you guess the nickname scientists have given the markings at the bottom?

Hint: it's a many-legged creepy-crawly.

VENUS

Although similar in size to Earth, Venus is very different. The temperature on Venus is hotter than an oven. The atmosphere is filled with poisonous gas. Its thick clouds of acid cause rain that would burn living things.

Venus's clouds are stinky, as well as toxic! Cross out all the letters in the cloud which appear three times to spell out what they smell like.

LROLLTBBTEBN ECCCGZGZSZ

_ _ _ _ _ _ _   _ _ _ _

Some scientists think that Venus may create powerful lightning in its toxic clouds. Can you count all the lightning bolts?

▪ Venus spins in a clockwise direction. This is the opposite direction to most of the other planets, including Earth.

At around 464 °C (867 °F), Venus is the hottest planet in the Solar System. It's hot enough to melt lead!
The thick atmosphere on Venus traps heat on the surface.

Complete this sudoku by placing one of each picture into every row, column, and minigrid.

- The surface of Venus is covered with more than 85,000 volcanoes—more than any other place in the Solar System.

- Amazingly, a day on Venus is equal to 117 Earth days! This is because it takes longer to spin on its axis than it does to travel once around the Sun.

- Venus can be seen easily with the naked eye, because its thick atmosphere reflects most of the sunlight that hits it. After the Sun and Moon, Venus is the brightest object in our skies.

SURFACE OF VENUS

Although it's much too deadly for people to visit, many space probes have explored Venus. They have mapped out the surface of Venus and made important discoveries.

Can you find all the space probes listed below in the word search?

Akatsuki
Vega
Magellan
Venera
Mariner
Venus Express
Pioneer

S	I	F	B	A	O	F	I	Q	Q	A	B
A	S	N	A	L	L	E	G	A	M	R	V
P	K	E	T	K	L	Q	P	F	Y	E	Y
I	B	A	R	E	Q	G	Q	P	J	N	X
O	Z	E	T	P	M	A	R	I	N	E	R
N	G	U	R	S	X	A	K	C	I	V	F
E	Q	N	G	G	U	E	W	G	W	A	A
E	N	U	T	A	U	K	S	Z	L	D	J
R	K	Y	G	U	N	C	I	U	O	Q	H
D	F	E	W	Q	M	Z	E	T	N	J	K
O	V	Q	J	T	I	P	P	O	K	E	W
K	O	Z	A	E	O	G	F	K	C	Y	V

▪ Mariner 2 completed the first successful flyby of any planet when it passed Venus in 1962.

▪ The Venera 13 probe landed on Venus in 1982. It took images of the surface for around two hours before it was destroyed by extreme heat and pressure.

Magellan was the first space probe to collect images of the entire surface of Venus. The largest crater Magellan pictured on Venus is the Mead Crater, which is 275 km (171 miles) wide.

Put the picture pieces in the correct order to reveal the Mead Crater.

1								9
1	2	3	4	5	6	7	8	9

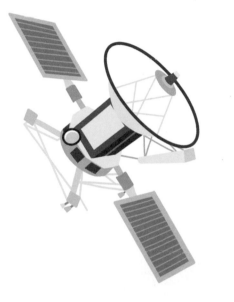

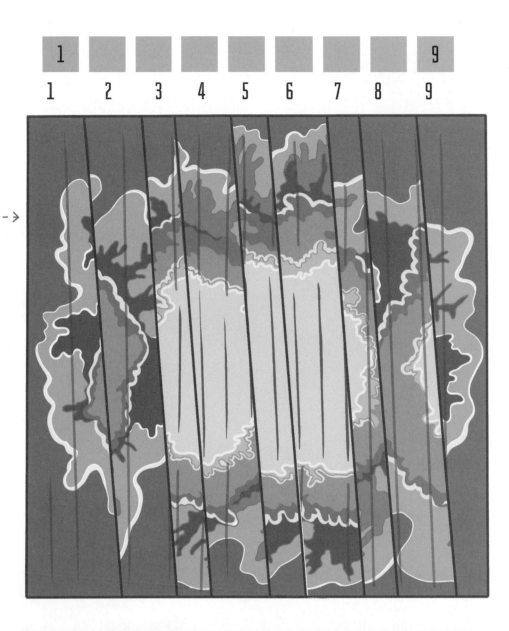

Can you work out which feature of Venus should come next in these sequences?

1

2

3

23

EARTH

Our home planet is unique in the Solar System. More than two-thirds of its rocky surface is covered with liquid water. It's also the only place we know of where life exists.

Can you find five differences between these two pictures of Earth's surface?

- The mixture of gases that surrounds a planet is called its atmosphere. Earth's atmosphere stops it getting too hot, or too cold, and helps protect it from space objects.

- Water, including oceans, lakes, and rivers, covers around 70% of the surface of Earth.

- Land covers about 30% of Earth's surface. The landscape includes mountains, deserts, and forests.

- The top layer of Earth is called the crust. Most of the crust is made up of rock, stone, and soil.

When viewed from space, Earth looks like a bright blue ball. Earth's oceans, land masses, and clouds can be seen clearly.

Look at pictures of Earth below. Can you find the odd one out?

A   B   C   D   E   F   G

Can you guess which of these statements about Earth is true or false?

1. Earth is the fourth planet from the Sun.
2. It takes Earth just over 365 days to orbit the Sun once.
3. Earth's seven large land masses are called the continents.
4. Oxygen makes up about 80% of the Earth's atmosphere.

THE RECIPE FOR LIFE

As far as we know, Earth is the only place in the Solar System that can support life. There are a few vital "ingredients" that make life possible on Earth.

- The Sun provides a constant source of heat and light. Earth is kept at the perfect temperature for life to exist.

- Without water in the form of oceans, rivers, ice, and rain, life would not be possible.

How many of each of these living things can you count in the scene?

■ Chemical elements essential for life
such as oxygen, nitrogen, and carbon are
found all over Earth—including in the air,
in water, and in soil.

OUR CHANGING PLANET

Earth is more than 4.5 billion years old. Over this time, the surface of our planet has changed a great deal.

Can you match these images of Earth to the correct descriptions?

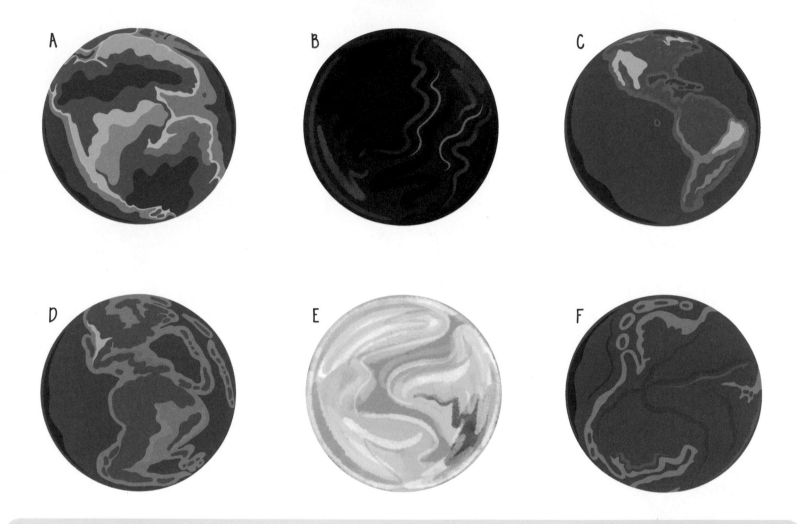

A

B

C

D

E

F

1. About 4 billion years ago, the surface of the young Earth was covered with molten rock.

2. Around 900 million years ago, Earth's surface was made up of a huge supercontinent, surrounded by one vast ocean.

3. Nicknamed "snowball Earth," much of the planet was covered with ice around 650 million years ago.

4. While dinosaurs walked the Earth, a supercontinent called Pangaea began to break apart.

5. Today, Earth's surface is made up of seven continents and five oceans.

6. In the future, some of Earth's continents could break apart, and others push together.

Earth is changing at a much quicker rate than ever before. Scientists studying Earth's atmosphere, land, ocean, and ice have concluded that the climate is getting warmer.

- There are some greenhouse gases in the atmosphere naturally. They help to keep our planet warm.

- Burning fossil fuels, such as oil and coal, creates more greenhouse gases in the air. This causes too much warming and damages the environment.

Greenhouse gases are chemicals that trap heat in the atmosphere. Use the code wheel to reveal one of the greenhouse gases that is warming Earth.

6 4 8 9 1 3   2 5 1 10 5 2 7

_ _ _ _ _ _   _ _ _ _ _ _ _

MARS

Around half the size of Earth, Mars is the fourth planet from the Sun. It is often called the Red Planet, because of its rusty-looking surface.

Work out the sum, solving it in order from left to right, then write the answer in the space in the sentence below.

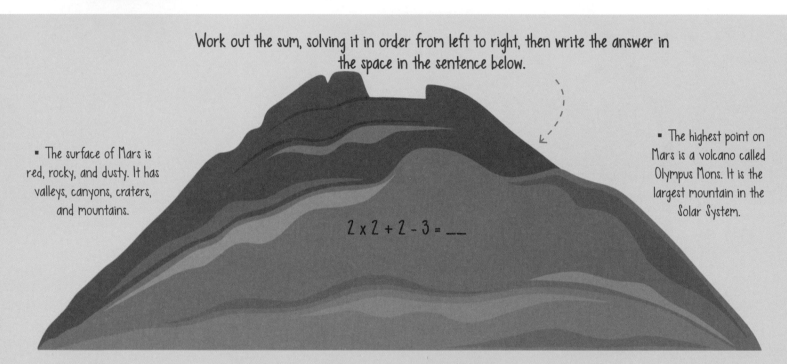

• The surface of Mars is red, rocky, and dusty. It has valleys, canyons, craters, and mountains.

• The highest point on Mars is a volcano called Olympus Mons. It is the largest mountain in the Solar System.

$2 \times 2 + 2 - 3 =$ ___

Olympus Mons is nearly ___ times higher than Mount Everest.

True or False?

It takes Mars almost twice as long to travel around the Sun as Earth does.

True   False

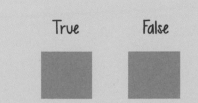

Mars has twin moons, called Phobos and Deimos. Match each
Phobos with a Deimos. Which moon is left over?

PHOBOS

DEIMOS

- The unusual-shaped Phobos and Deimos may have been
  asteroids that were pulled into orbit by Mars' gravity.

- Deimos is the smallest of Mars' moons. It is about
  15 km (9 miles) at its widest point.

- The moons get their names from Greek mythology.
  Phobos means "fear" and Deimos means "terror."

EXPLORING MARS

Other than Earth, Mars is the most explored planet in our Solar System. Mars is studied from space, and on the ground. Rovers are robotic vehicles which travel the surface taking photos and collecting information.

FINISH

1.

Follow this sequence of tracks to help the rover find its way across Mars. You can move up, down, left, and right—but not diagonally.

2.

3.

- The first Mars rover was Sojourner, which landed in 1997. It was about the size of a microwave oven.

START

- The twin rovers Spirit and Opportunity gathered evidence that water once flowed on Mars.

- The Curiosity rover is about the size of a car. It is remote-controlled by a team of scientists on Earth.

The Perseverance rover landed on Mars in 2021. It has seven science instruments on board and is searching for signs of past life.

Look at this scene and read the facts below. Then turn the page to see what you can remember.

- Perseverance landed on an area of Mars called the Jezero Crater.

- The rover is collecting soil and rock samples, which will eventually be brought back to Earth to study.

- Perseverance came to Mars carrying a small helicopter called Ingenuity.

- Technology onboard Perseverance is designed to produce oxygen from carbon dioxide in the Martian atmosphere.

Answer the questions below to find out how much you remember about the Perseverance rover.

1. How many wheels does Perseverance have?
2. Which gas has Perseverance produced?
3. What type of samples is Perseverance collecting?
4. Which part of Mars did Perseverance land on?
5. What is the name of the helicopter that was carried by Perseverance?

One day humans will walk on the surface of Mars. The company SpaceX plans to send people to Mars in its Starship space craft.

Which route should Starship take to reach Mars? ___

A   B   C   D

Like Earth, Mars has seasons and weather. However, Mars is cold and dry, with a thin and toxic atmosphere.

Mars is known for its powerful wind storms that create huge clouds of dust and can last for weeks.
Which puzzle pieces fit into the picture?

A

B

C

D

- Due to strong winds and other conditions on Mars, sand dunes are much bigger than any found on Earth.

Dust devils are whirlwinds that whip over the Martian desert. How many dust devils can you count?

- Mars has around a third of the gravity of Earth. If you dropped a ball on Mars, it would fall more slowly than it would on Earth. It would also weigh less!

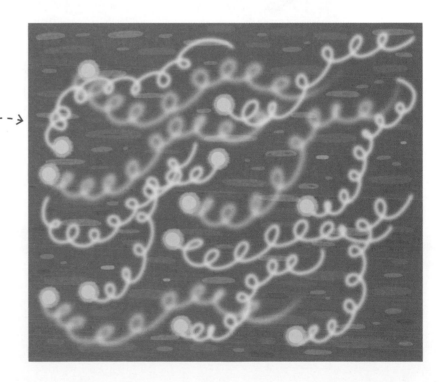

THE OUTER PLANETS

The four planets farthest from the Sun are the gas giants Jupiter, Saturn, Uranus, and Neptune. These huge planets have small rocky cores, covered with layers of liquid and gas.

JUPITER

Named after the king of the Roman gods, Jupiter is the largest planet in the Solar System. Jupiter is so huge that more than 1,300 Earth-sized planets could fit inside.

Jupiter is famous for its Great Red Spot, which is around 16,000 km (10,000 miles) wide. Look at the pictures below. Can you find the odd spot out?

A

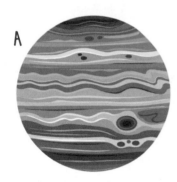

- Jupiter's Great Red Spot is a huge swirling storm, a bit like a hurricane.

B

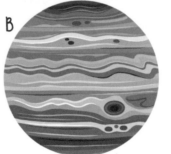

- The spot moves around, sucking up other storms as it goes.

C

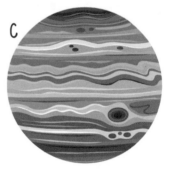

- The Great Red Spot is getting smaller. It is half the size it was 100 years ago.

D

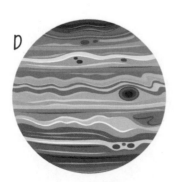

E

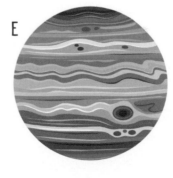

- The storm's winds blow at around 500 km/h (310 mph).

Jupiter can be seen easily from Earth with the naked eye. If you look through a telescope, you'll see Jupiter's beautiful markings.

- Jupiter's stripes are bands of tinted clouds which swirl around the planet.

- Scientists think the clouds are made of water and the chemical ammonia.

Complete this picture of Jupiter, making sure you add the stripes and Great Red Spot.

- Most of Jupiter is freezing cold gases, but its solid core may be six times hotter than the Sun's surface!

Jupiter spins faster than any other planet in the Solar System, which means its days are short.

Solve the number problem to find out how long a Jupiter day is in Earth hours.

9 + 7 - 6 = ___

JUPITER'S MOONS

Gas planets usually have lots of moons, and Jupiter is no exception. Jupiter has around 95 moons—
perhaps more. The four largest moons were first spotted by the scientist Galileo in 1610.

How many of Jupiter's moons can
you count in the main scene? ____

A

B

■ As well as moons, Jupiter has four faint rings,
which cannot be seen from Earth.

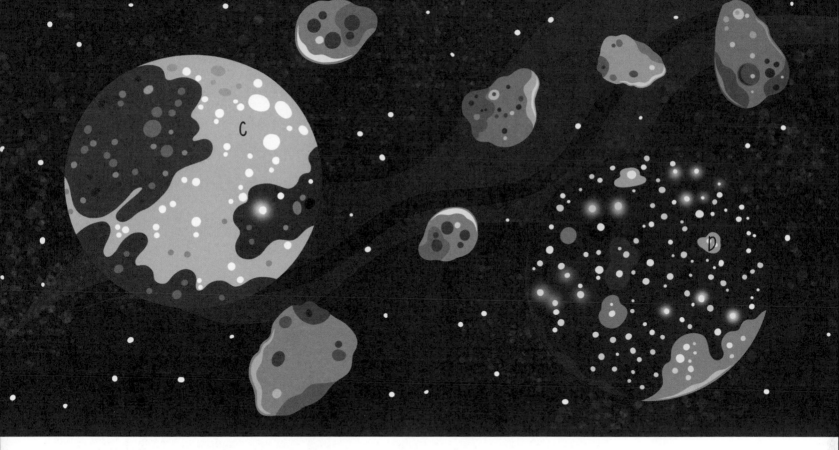

Match Jupiter's Galilean moons to the images in the main picture.

Write the correct letters in the boxes.

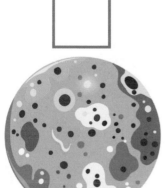

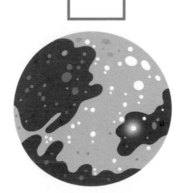

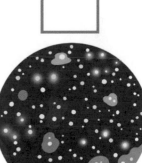

Io is about the same size as Earth's Moon. It is covered with erupting volcanoes.

Europa could contain simple life forms in the ocean below its icy surface.

Ganymede is the largest moon in the Solar System. It is bigger than Mercury.

Callisto is like a huge ball of dusty ice, covered with craters.

SATURN

Gas giant Saturn is one of the most iconic planets in the Solar System. It is the second largest planet, and is known for its huge rings.

• The Cassini spacecraft spent 13 years orbiting Saturn. It sent back beautiful images of Saturn's rings and icy moons.

Cassini sent a probe called Huygens onto Saturn's largest moon. Rearrange the letters to spell the moon's name.

TANIT

_ _ _ _ _

Which of these statements about Saturn are true, and which are false?

	TRUE	FALSE
1. Saturn's rings were only discovered 20 years ago.	☐	☐
2. One day, people will walk on the surface of Saturn.	☐	☐
3. Like Jupiter, Saturn is mostly made up of hydrogen and helium gases.	☐	☐
4. Saturn's moon Titan is the largest in the Solar System.	☐	☐
5. A year on Saturn is the equivalent of approximately 29 Earth years.	☐	☐

Can you find your way through the maze of Saturn's rings?

START

FINISH

- Saturn is very light for its size. If you could put Saturn in an enormous tub of water it would float.

- There are gaps between the rings where Saturn's moons orbit.

- Saturn has 66 named moons and 80 more that are still to be named.

THE RINGS OF SATURN

Other planets have rings, but Saturn's sparkling rings are the biggest, brightest, and most impressive in the Solar System. The rings are more than 280,000 km (175,000 miles) wide, but only 10 m (30 ft) thick.

Look at the picture of Saturn, then match the puzzle pieces to the correct places.

Can you work out which jigsaw piece doesn't fit?

1

2

3

4

A

B

C

- Saturn's rings are HUGE. From edge to edge, the ring system measures more than the distance between the Earth and the Moon.

- Each of Saturn's rings orbits the planet at a different speed.

How many of Saturn's rings can be seen from Earth? Count the rings to find out: _____

Saturn's rings are made up of billions of particles of ice and rock. Some particles are thought to be broken-up pieces of asteroids, comets, and moons, which were shattered by Saturn's gravity.

Complete the sudoku with some of the things that make up Saturn's rings. Every row, column, and minigrid should contain just one of each picture.

Asteroid

Comet

Moon

Ice

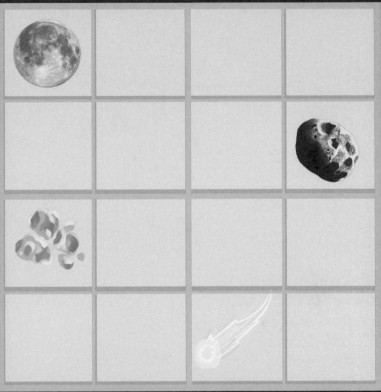

Look at the five pictures of Saturn below. Can you spot the odd one out?

▪ The particles range in size from mountain-sized chunks, to teeny-tiny grains of ice and dust.

A

B

D

C

E

▪ Although Saturn formed around 4.5 billion years ago, its rings are much younger. The rings formed no more than 100 million years ago, when dinosaurs lived on Earth.

▪ If you were looking down from the very top of Saturn, the rings would appear white.

URANUS

Known as an ice giant as well as a gas giant, Uranus is the Solar System's coldest planet. Its atmosphere contains clouds of methane which gives Uranus its shade of blue.

Uranus was discovered in 1781 by William Herschel. It was the first planet to be discovered with a telescope.

Join the dots to reveal Herschel's telescope.

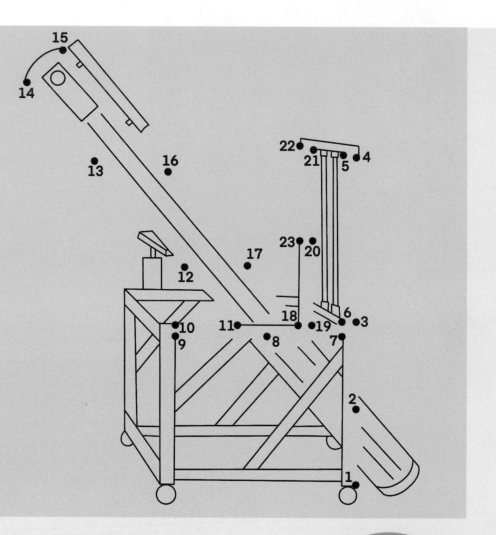

• Titania is Uranus' largest moon.

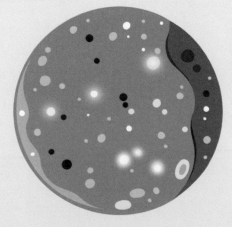

Uranus has around 27 moons. Most of them are named after characters in plays by a well-known writer. Fill in the missing letters to spell his name.

W_LL_ _M SH_K_SP_ _R_

44

Uranus has rings, circling the planet from top to bottom. Using the picture on the opposite page, add rings to the outline of Uranus. One ring has been added for you. Use your brightest shades of blue!

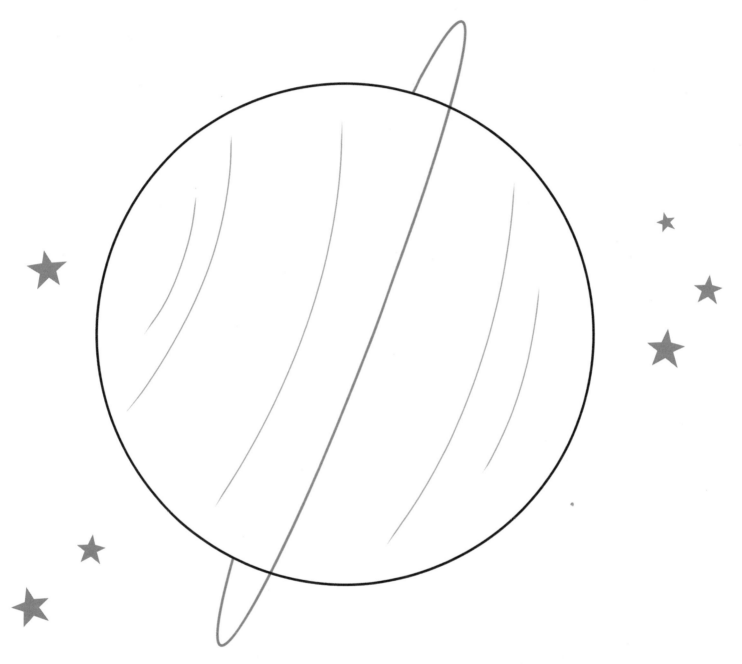

When Herschel first spotted Uranus, he didn't know the planet had rings.

Cross out all the even numbers, then write the leftover numbers in the box to complete the sentence.

2144964782722

Uranus' rings were discovered in ____.

UNUSUAL URANUS

Uranus is the only planet that spins on its side like a rolling ball. Experts believe that an object the size of Earth smashed into Uranus and knocked it over.

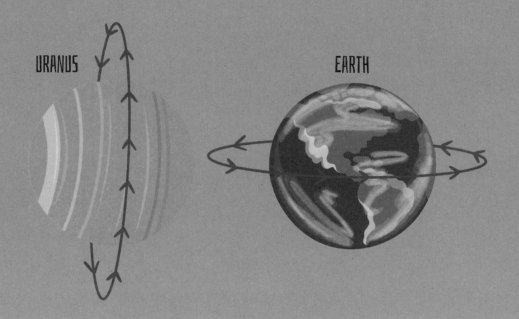

URANUS

EARTH

How many pictures of Uranus can you count in this jumble? Can you spot the Uranus which is the wrong way round?

Uranus spins in the opposite way to all the other planets—except one. Can you remember which one?

Voyager 2 is the first and only spacecraft to ever fly past Uranus.
Can you spot five differences between the two pictures?

- Voyager 2 launched in 1977 to study the four gas planets.

- In 1986 Voyager reached Uranus and flew through its rings.

- Voyager 2 discovered ten new moons and two new rings.

- Scientists think that Uranus has fewer storms than other gas giants.

Which of these features did Voyager 2 find evidence for on Uranus?

A. A massive volcano

B. A dusty desert

C. A boiling ocean

NEPTUNE

Way out at the edge of the solar system is the windy world of Neptune. Like Uranus, Neptune is an ice giant. It is the farthest planet from the Sun, and is very cold and dark.

After its flyby of Uranus, Voyager 2 flew on to study Neptune. Can you work out which flightpath Voyager 2 should take to reach Neptune?

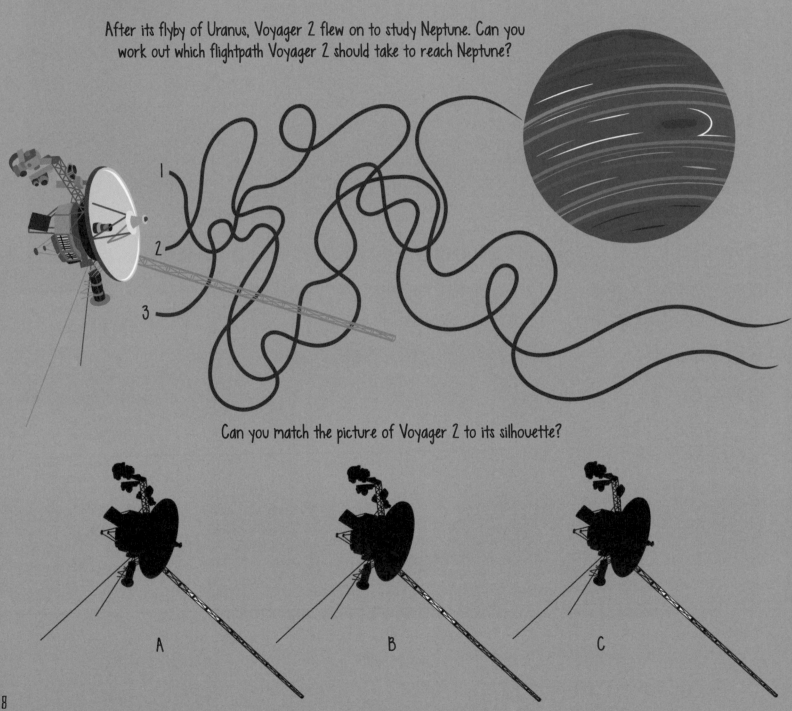

1

2

3

Can you match the picture of Voyager 2 to its silhouette?

A

B

C

When Voyager 2 flew past Neptune, it took pictures of methane clouds and a huge Earth-sized storm.

Use the code wheel to work out the name given to the storm:

• Neptune is thought to be the windiest planet in the Solar System.

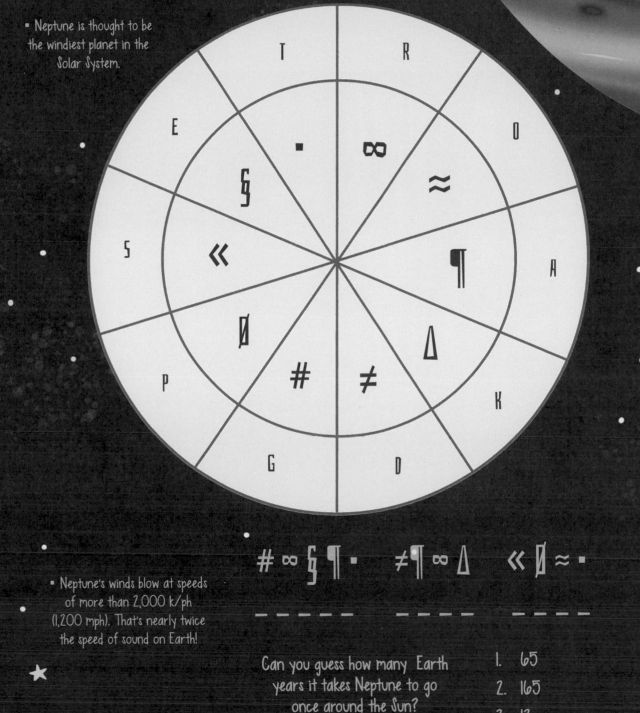

∞ § ¶ ·   ≠ ¶ ∞ Δ   « Ø ≈ ·

_ _ _ _ _   _ _ _ _   _ _ _ _

• Neptune's winds blow at speeds of more than 2,000 k/ph (1,200 mph). That's nearly twice the speed of sound on Earth!

Can you guess how many Earth years it takes Neptune to go once around the Sun?

1. 65
2. 165
3. 12

ICY BLUE PLANET

With a cloud-top temperature of −200 °C (−330 °F) Neptune is a very cold and stormy place. However, Neptune's largest moon Triton is colder even than Neptune.

On the surface of Triton, freezing geysers and "cryovolcanoes" spew out ice and gases. Add some more ice geysers to Triton's frosty surface.

- The temperature on Triton is -235 °C (-391 °F). It may be the coldest object in the Solar System.

- Neptune has 14 moons and six rings. The rings are very faint and difficult to see.

- Neptune appears dark blue because of the methane in its atmosphere.

Scientists believe that deep down on Neptune and Uranus it might rain diamonds! This is partly because of the mix of chemicals and high pressure inside the planets.

Can you work out which diamond comes next in these sequences?

Complete this gas giant sudoku. A planet must appear only once in each row, column, and minigrid.

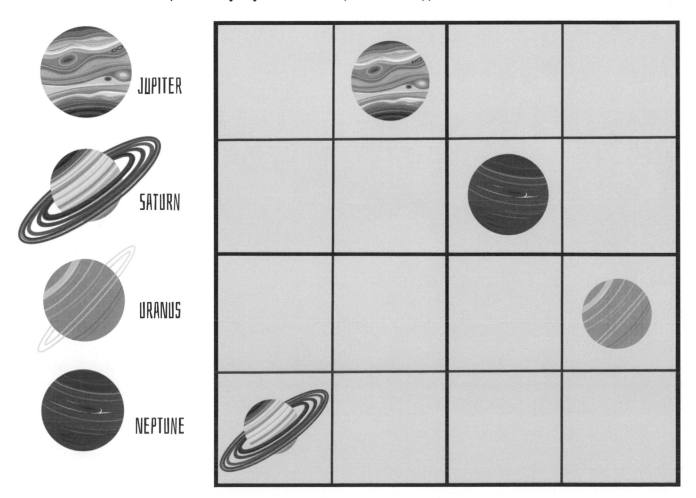

JUPITER

SATURN

URANUS

NEPTUNE

There are not just the planets and their moons in the Solar System. There are also billions of rocky objects, such as asteroids, meteoroids, dwarf planets, and comets.

THE ASTEROID BELT

There is a band of rocky objects that orbits the Sun between Mars and Jupiter. Called the Asteroid Belt, it contains most of the asteroids in our Solar System.

Match the jigsaw pieces to the correct places on the picture. Which two pieces do not belong?

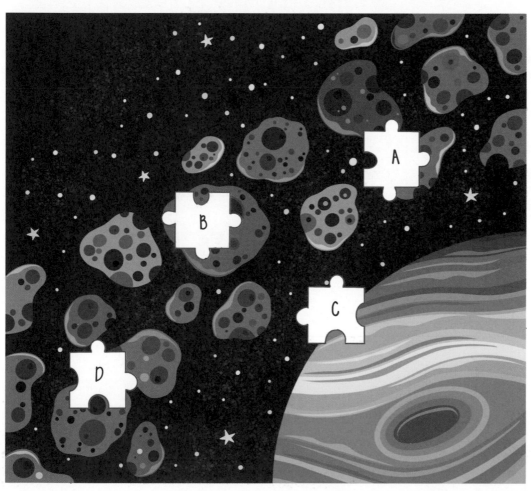

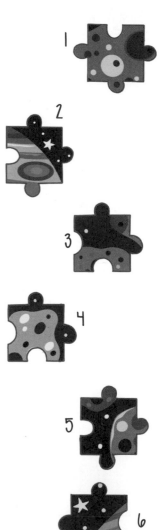

▪ There are almost 2 million asteroids more than 1 km (0.6 miles) long in the asteroid belt. There are many millions of smaller rocky fragments.

▪ If you could collect up all fragments in the asteroid belt, it would create an object almost the size of our Moon.

The Asteroid Belt also contains a dwarf planet. It's the only one to be found here, as dwarf planets are usually located at the edges of the Solar System.

Complete the word search by finding each rocky object in the grid. The word from the list that cannot be found in the grid is the name of the dwarf planet in the Asteroid Belt.

B	D	U	B	C	S	T	I	D	C
E	A	C	F	D	E	G	E	R	O
F	H	S	I	G	I	C	E	H	J
K	M	E	T	E	O	R	O	I	D
I	L	J	C	E	K	K	M	K	L
N	M	R	O	N	R	E	O	T	P
P	Q	O	R	A	F	O	Y	S	E
H	S	C	O	Y	E	S	I	U	T
U	M	K	E	V	T	E	O	D	W
X	O	I	Y	D	D	Z	U	S	A

ASTEROID
DUST
ICE
CERES
METEOROID
ROCK

■ Trojan asteroids are two groups of asteroids that are trapped in orbit with Jupiter around the Sun.

ASTEROIDS

Space rocks come in many different shapes and sizes. Scientists group asteroids according to what they are made of. The three main groups are C-type, S-type, and M-type asteroids.

Can you sort these asteroids into their groups, by matching each picture to its description?

1

2

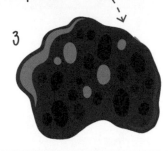

3

S-type asteroids are bright, stony and contain some metal.

M-type asteroids are made of metal, and can look reddish-brown due to the iron content.

C-type asteroids are dark and stony. They are the most common type of asteroid.

Asteroids are regularly being discovered and named. Can you find each of the asteroids in this word search?

BENNU   JUNO
FORTUNA   NEMESIS
GASPRA   PALLAS
HERMIONE   SYLVIA
IDA   VESTA

- Scientists think a massive asteroid hit Earth 66 million years ago, wiping out the dinosaurs.

- Ida has its own moon, called Dactyl. The moon was probably once a part of Ida that was knocked off by another asteroid.

A	G	Y	A	K	P	A	N	D	N
I	R	D	M	A	Y	N	M	H	E
V	I	J	L	Z	X	U	Y	E	M
L	G	L	V	E	S	T	A	R	E
Y	A	W	K	K	Q	R	E	M	S
S	U	R	C	O	K	O	E	I	I
P	N	E	Q	N	I	F	B	O	S
D	N	M	K	U	U	P	D	N	A
P	E	M	B	J	S	H	Q	E	P
B	B	M	B	G	A	S	P	R	A

In 2020 the OSIRIS–REx spacecraft landed on the asteroid Bennu. It collected a sample of the asteroid to be brought back to Earth and studied by scientists.

Can you spot five differences between these two pictures?

- Bennu is around 492 m (1,614 ft) wide. It contains the precious metals gold and platinum.

- It took OSIRIS-REx two years to reach Bennu.

- After it has delivered the sample from Bennu to Earth, OSIRIS-REx will visit another asteroid called Apophis.

- Scientists use powerful telescopes to watch out for asteroids that may come close to Earth.

METEOROIDS

When rocky objects collide with each other, smaller pieces can break off. These pieces are called meteoroids. Most meteoroids come from asteroids, or comets.

Read the facts around the page, then look at the picture. How many meteoroids, meteors, and meteorites can you count?

- Meteoroids are rocks in space that are smaller than asteroids.

- Meteors are meteoroids that burn up as they fall through a planet's atmosphere. They look like a streak of light in the sky.

- Meteorites are meteoroids that make it through the atmosphere and hit the ground.

Meteoroids ___   Meteors ___   Meteorites ___

Every day, around a million meteors can be seen from Earth. Sometimes a lot of meteors fall at once, creating what is called a meteor shower.

Complete this picture by adding some meteors to the sky.

• Meteors are sometimes called shooting stars, because of the bright trails they make in the sky.

• Meteor showers happen at certain times of the year. They are usually made up of small particles from comets.

• The Perseids meteor shower happens in the summer. At its peak, up to 80 meteors an hour can be seen.

A meteorite has been spotted in the desert. Follow the directions to find its location, then draw it in the correct square.

Start at square A1.

Go right two squares.

Go up three squares.

Go right two squares.

Go down one square.

Go left one square.

Meteorite location: ___

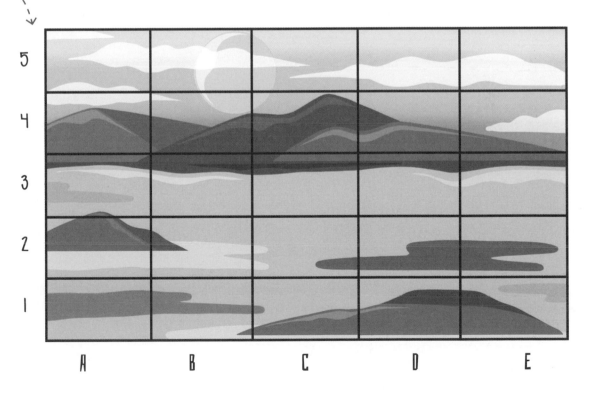

DWARF PLANETS

Some rocky bodies have things in common with planets, but they are not massive enough to be called planets. The most well-known dwarf planet is Pluto. Pluto is a very cold place. Along with most dwarf planets, Pluto is found on the edge of the Solar System, in an area called the Kuiper Belt.

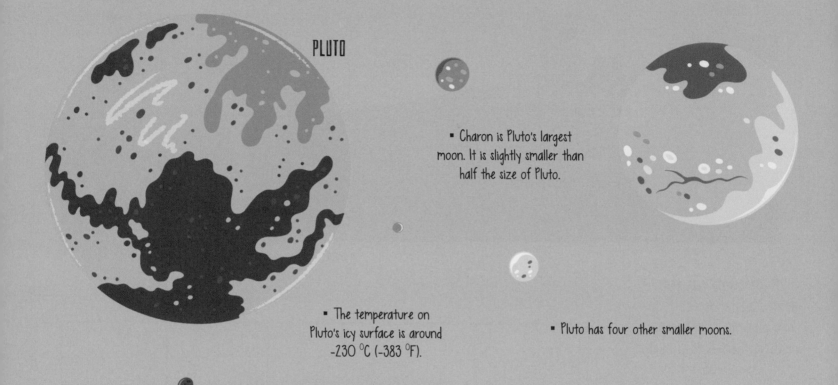

PLUTO

- Charon is Pluto's largest moon. It is slightly smaller than half the size of Pluto.

- The temperature on Pluto's icy surface is around -230 °C (-383 °F).

- Pluto has four other smaller moons.

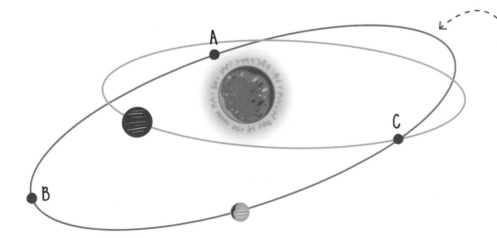

Pluto's orbit around the Sun is long and oval shaped. Look at the points marked A, B, and C on the picture which shows the Sun, Neptune, and Pluto, then answer the questions.

1. Which point shows Pluto farthest from the Sun? ___

2. Which point shows Pluto closer to the Sun than to Neptune? ___

3. Which point shows Pluto and Neptune at the same distance from the Sun? ___

There are four other named dwarf planets, but probably many more to be discovered.

Take a look at these fact files, then turn the book upside down and see if you can answer all the questions at the top.

NAME: Makemake
LOCATION: Kuiper Belt
SIZE: 1,500 km (900 miles) across
DID YOU KNOW? It takes Makemake around 305 Earth years to orbit the Sun.

Name: Ceres
LOCATION: Asteroid Belt
SIZE: 940 km (580 miles) across

DID YOU KNOW? Ceres is the only dwarf planet to be found in the Asteroid Belt.

NAME: HAUMEA
LOCATION: Kuiper Belt
SIZE: 2,100 km (1,300 miles) long
DID YOU KNOW? Haumea is shaped like a squashed rugby ball, or American football.

Name: Eris
LOCATION: Kuiper Belt
SIZE: 2,326 km (1,445 miles) across

DID YOU KNOW? As far as we know now, Eris is the dwarf planet farthest from the Sun.

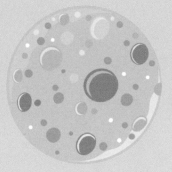

4. Which dwarf planet has the most unusual shape?

3. Which dwarf planet is the smallest?

2. Which dwarf planet has an orbit of 305 Earth years?

1. Which dwarf planet is the farthest from the Sun?

COMETS

Like giant snowballs zooming through space, comets are made of frozen gases, rock, and dust.
Their oval-shaped orbits around the Sun can take hundreds of years.

As they get closer to the Sun, comets heat up and gases and dust stream behind them in two long "tails."
Follow the comet trails to find out which telescope spots the comet.

A

B

C

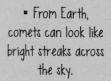

• From Earth, comets can look like bright streaks across the sky.

• The only solid part of a comet is its core, called the nucleus.

• In 1994, a comet named Shoemaker-Levy 9 crashed into Jupiter.

Comets are named after the person, people, or the equipment that discovered them. The most well-known comet is Halley's Comet, which was named after the English astronomer Edmund Halley in the 1700s.

an you spot all
se comets in the
t sky? Tick them
you find them.

Comet McNaught, seen in 2006, had an amazing curved dust tail.

Comet Hale-Bopp was seen with the naked eye for 18 months in the 1990s.

Comet Halley is visible from Earth every 76 years.

Comet NEOWISE was discovered using a space telescope in 2020.

How many comets can you see in total? ___

THE MOON

A moon is a natural satellite that orbits another object in space. There are hundreds of moons in our Solar System. Some of the gas giant planets have dozens of moons, but Earth has only one.

MANY MOONS

Planets, dwarf planets, and even asteroids can have moons. Moons come in many different shapes and sizes. They are not all round, like Earth's Moon.

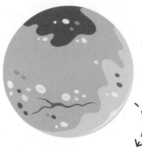

Charon is about half the size of the dwarf planet it orbits.

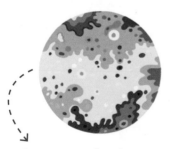

Io is covered with volcanoes. It orbits the largest planet in the Solar System.

Hyperion is an unusual-looking moon that belongs to a gas giant.

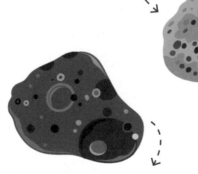

Phobos is the largest of the twin moons that orbits the Red Planet.

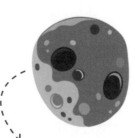

Dactyl is a tiny moon that orbits an asteroid.

Flick back through the book to help you!

Draw lines to match each object with its moon.

Jupiter

Mars

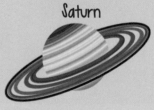

Saturn

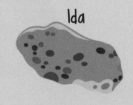

Ida

Pluto

62

Look at this scene and read the facts below. Then turn the page to see what you can remember.

- It may look like it shines, but the Moon does not produce any light of its own. The Moon glows at night because it reflects light from the Sun.

- The Moon is the closest natural object in space to our home planet.

- At around 3,475 km (2,159 miles) across, the Moon is about a quarter of the size of Earth.

- The Moon is about 384,400 km (238,855 miles) away from Earth. That's a distance of about 30 Earths.

Answer the questions below to find out how much you remember about the Moon.

1. What is the closest natural object in space to Earth?
2. How many Earths would fit between Earth and the Moon?
3. What is on the lake?
4. Why does the Moon glow?
5. How many birds are in the sky?

The Moon formed billions of years ago. Scientists believe an object the size of Mars crashed into Earth, knocking off fragments. Over time, the fragments came together, forming the Moon.

Which three pieces would make a complete picture of the Moon?

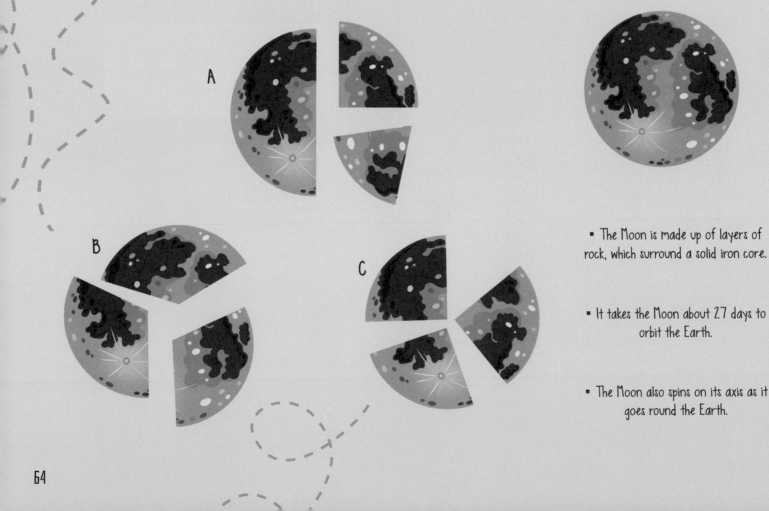

- The Moon is made up of layers of rock, which surround a solid iron core.

- It takes the Moon about 27 days to orbit the Earth.

- The Moon also spins on its axis as it goes round the Earth.

PHASES OF THE MOON

The Moon appears to change shape because, as it orbits Earth, different parts are lit up by the Sun. It takes about a month for the Moon to complete its cycle.

Shade in each of the pictures according to its description of the Moon. Shade the dark part and leave the rest of the Moon white.

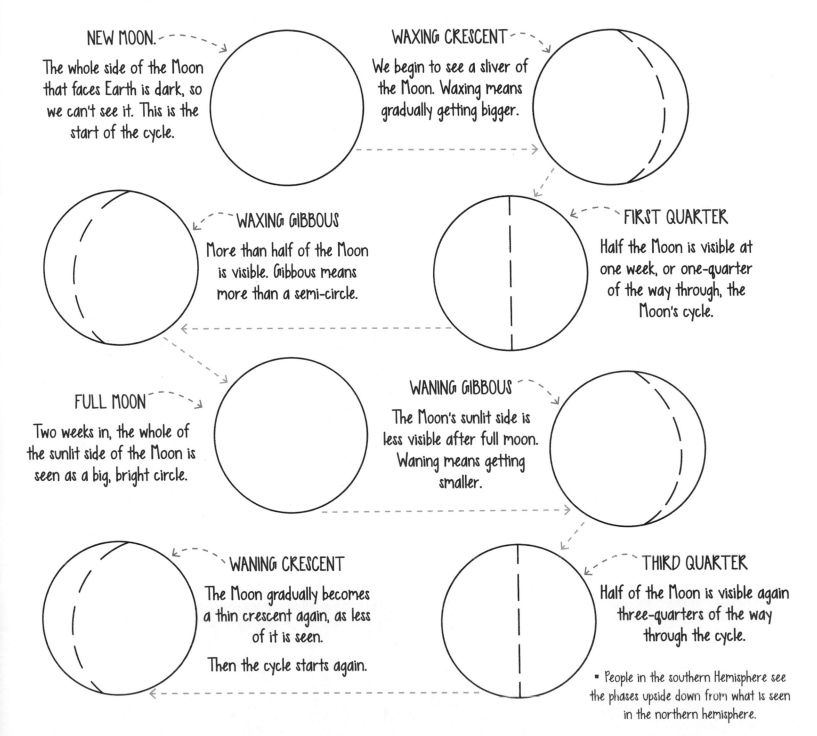

NEW MOON.

The whole side of the Moon that faces Earth is dark, so we can't see it. This is the start of the cycle.

WAXING CRESCENT

We begin to see a sliver of the Moon. Waxing means gradually getting bigger.

WAXING GIBBOUS

More than half of the Moon is visible. Gibbous means more than a semi-circle.

FIRST QUARTER

Half the Moon is visible at one week, or one-quarter of the way through, the Moon's cycle.

FULL MOON

Two weeks in, the whole of the sunlit side of the Moon is seen as a big, bright circle.

WANING GIBBOUS

The Moon's sunlit side is less visible after full moon. Waning means getting smaller.

WANING CRESCENT

The Moon gradually becomes a thin crescent again, as less of it is seen.

Then the cycle starts again.

THIRD QUARTER

Half of the Moon is visible again three-quarters of the way through the cycle.

▪ People in the southern Hemisphere see the phases upside down from what is seen in the northern hemisphere.

ECLIPSES

Sometimes an object in space lines up with the Sun and blocks the sunlight shining on another object. This is called an eclipse. An eclipse can be partial or total.

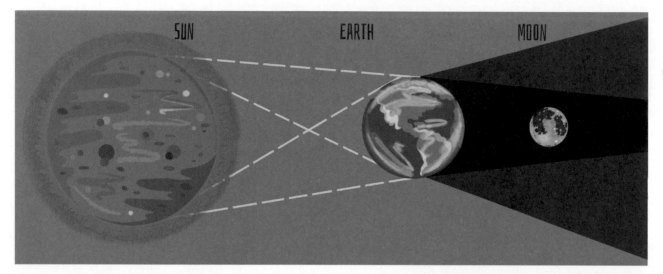

When the Earth lines up between the Sun and the Moon, it plunges the Moon into shadow. This is a lunar eclipse.

During a total lunar eclipse, the Moon can appear reddish-orange. Can you guess the name it is given?

1. Blood moon
2. Crimson moon
3. Tomato moon

- The Moon rotates at the same rate as it goes around the Earth, so we only ever see one side of the Moon.

Put the segments in the correct order to complete the picture.

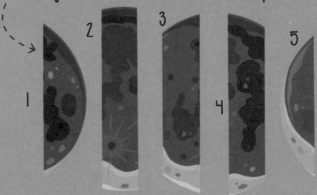

When the Moon lines up between the Earth and the Sun, it blocks out light from the Sun.
This is a solar eclipse.

A partial solar eclipse is when part of the Sun is blocked out. A total solar eclipse is when the whole Sun is covered. Can you find the total eclipse in the jumble of partial eclipses?

• A total eclipse can be seen somewhere from Earth's surface every 18 months.

It's important to use safety glasses when viewing solar eclipses. Match these safety glasses into pairs.
Which glasses do not have a matching pair?

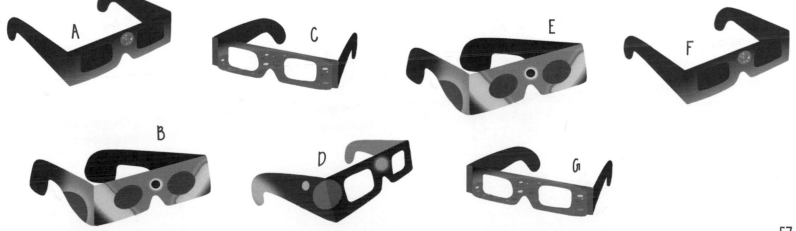

A

C

E

F

B

D

G

THE MOON'S SURFACE

If we look at the Moon, we can easily see that it's not a smooth white surface.
The Moon is pitted with hundreds of craters and many dark patches.

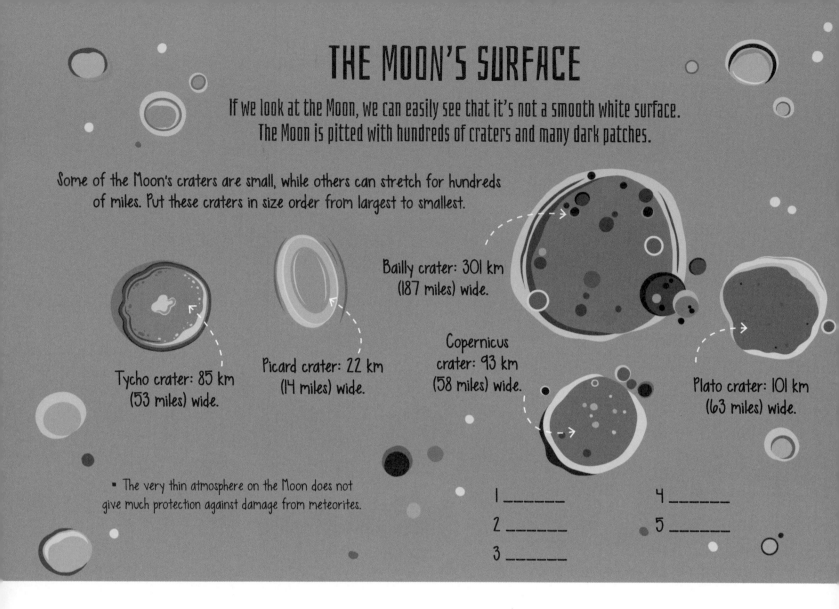

Some of the Moon's craters are small, while others can stretch for hundreds of miles. Put these craters in size order from largest to smallest.

Bailly crater: 301 km (187 miles) wide.

Copernicus crater: 93 km (58 miles) wide.

Tycho crater: 85 km (53 miles) wide.

Picard crater: 22 km (14 miles) wide.

Plato crater: 101 km (63 miles) wide.

• The very thin atmosphere on the Moon does not give much protection against damage from meteorites.

1 _____   4 _____

2 _____   5 _____

3 _____

The dark areas on the Moon's surface are called "seas." They formed when lava flowed from volcanoes and hardened on the surface. Can you spot the odd Moon out?

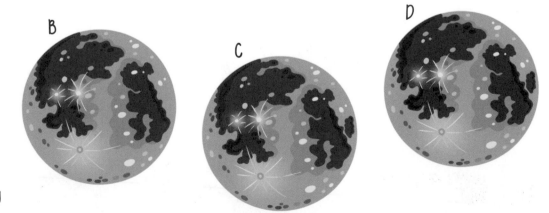

A

B

C

D

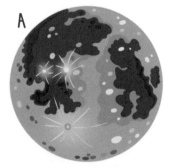

• The Sea of Tranquility was the landing site for the Apollo 11 mission in 1969.

The Moon is the only natural place in space that people have visited. In total, 12 people have walked on the surface.

Follow this sequence of astronaut footprints to find your way across the Moon's surface.

You can only move up, down, left, and right.

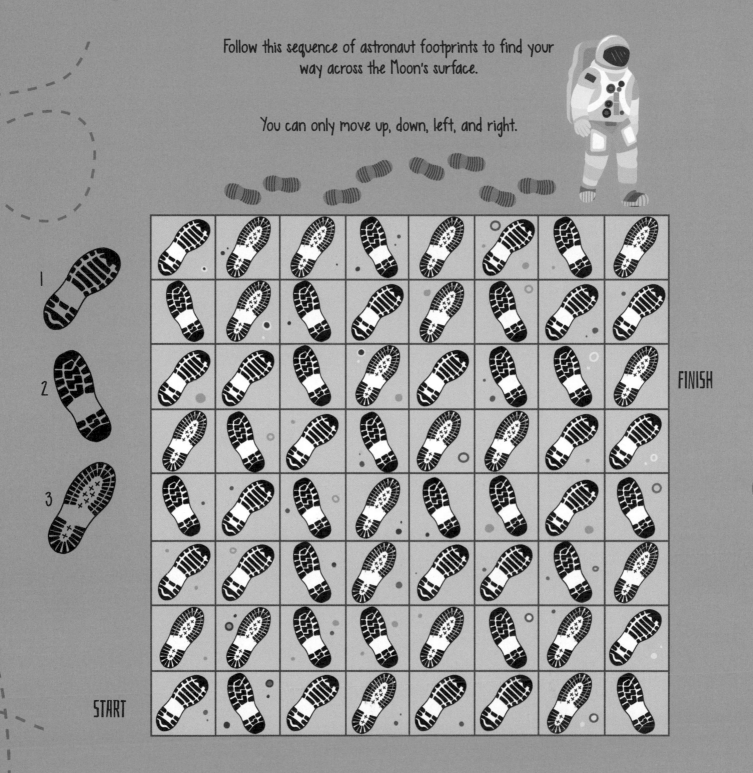

1

2

3

START

FINISH

* Because there is no wind on the Moon, astronauts' footprints will remain on the surface for millions of years to come.

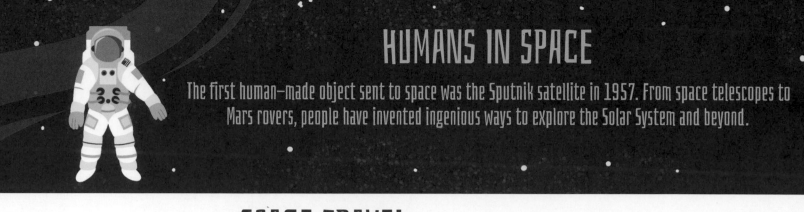

HUMANS IN SPACE

The first human-made object sent to space was the Sputnik satellite in 1957. From space telescopes to Mars rovers, people have invented ingenious ways to explore the Solar System and beyond.

SPACE TRAVEL

Russian astronaut Yuri Gagarin became the first person to go into space in 1961. He orbited Earth in the Vostok 1 spacecraft. There have been more than 300 manned space flight launches since then.

A

B

C

A "spacewalk" is when an astronaut goes outside a vehicle in space. Alexei Leonov completed the first spacewalk in 1965. Which spacewalking astronaut is attached to the spacecraft?

Complete the sum below to work out how many minutes Alexei Leonov's spacewalk lasted.

28 ÷ 2 - 2 = _____ minutes.

The Space Shuttle was the first reusable spacecraft. It first launched from the USA in 1981 and its last mission was in 2011.

Can you spot six differences between the two pictures of the Discovery Space Shuttle?

- The orbiter is the part that looks like a plane. The orbiter carried the astronauts and equipment.

- Space shuttles were used to launch satellites and space probes, and to take people and equipment to space stations.

- The farthest humans have been is when the Apollo 13 crew flew past the far side of the Moon—around 400,171 km (248, 655 miles) from Earth.

- Space probes are unmanned spacecraft. Voyager 1 is the first probe to travel beyond our Solar System.

MOON LANDINGS

In the 1950s and 1960s, the USA and Soviet Union (including Russia) were striving to be the first country to put people into space. This was known as the Space Race. Their goal was to send people to the Moon.

In 1957, the Soviet Union sent the first living creature into orbit. Can you guess which animal it was?

In 1969, the USA's Apollo 11 mission took astronauts to the Moon for the first time.

A. Cat

B. Mouse

C. Dog

Help Apollo 11 get through the maze to the Moon, making sure you pass every flag on the way.

START

FINISH

- Neil Armstrong and Buzz Aldrin were the first people to walk on the Moon's surface.

A total of 12 people landed on the Moon from 1969 to 1972. Astronauts used the Lunar Roving Vehicle, or LRV, during the last three Apollo missions. Follow the directions to find the LRV's location, then draw it in the correct square.

Start at square A1.

Go up two squares.

Go right three squares.

Go down one square.

Go right one square.

LRV location: ___

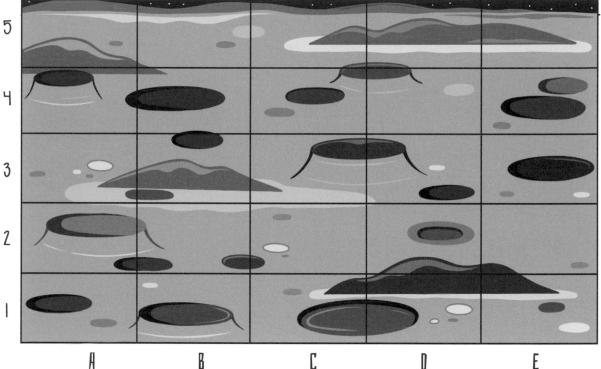

NASA's Artemis Program is sending people to the Moon for the first time in more than 50 years. Astronauts will travel on the Orion spacecraft.

Take a look at the steps and draw your own Orion spacecraft.

1

2

3

4

LIVING IN SPACE

The International Space Station (ISS) is a large spacecraft that orbits the Earth. Astronauts live and work on the space station. They gather data, conduct experiments, and repair equipment.

Living in space puts pressure on the body, so astronauts keep themselves healthy by exercising every day. Can you work out which astronaut exercised for the longest? _____

Brad

Maya

Yusuf

Brad ran on the treadmill for 1 hour, and cycled for 55 minutes.

Maya ran for 45 minutes, then did 90 minutes of weight-training.

Yusuf weight-trained for 1 hour and 5 minutes, followed by a 60-minute run.

Astronauts plant seeds in labs on the ISS to test how plants grow in space. Can you put these seedlings into matching pairs?

A

B

C

D

E

F

- In the future, astronauts may rely on growing plants for food during long space missions.

74

The International Space Station is the largest human-made object ever to be flown in space.
Join the dots to see what the ISS looks like. Then use your pens and pencils to finish the picture.

▪ The ISS orbits Earth at about 400 km (250 miles) above the surface.

36
29● ●30 35

▪ There is little gravity in space, making objects weightless. Astronauts use harnesses and magnets to keep equipment (and themselves!) from floating around.

34 37
31● ●
28●

9 ●10
3● 4

27 32 33 38
22 26 25 40 39
21 23 24 41 42
2● 5 8 ●11 20 43
19 44
18 45
1● 6 7 12 13 46
15 14
16 17 47

▪ Work done on the ISS helps scientists plan for space travel. It also improves our understanding of our own planet.

When astronauts work outside the ISS, they must wear thick, insulated spacesuits with oxygen packs to survive.

SATELLITES

Man-made satellites are machines that orbit a planet or other objects in space. There are currently more than 5,000 active satellites orbiting Earth.

Satellites come in different shapes and sizes, depending on their purpose. Draw lines to match these satellites to their silhouettes.

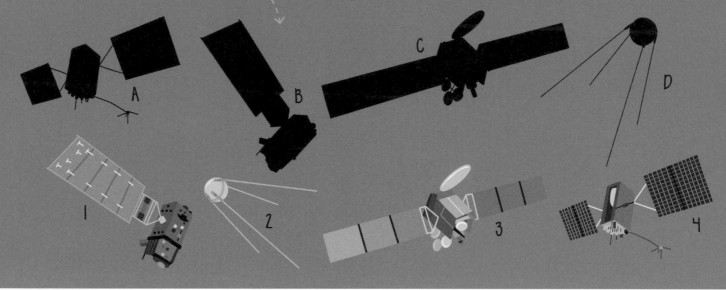

Many cars use GPS to help people plan a route. Use the directions to help the blue car reach its destination. Draw the location symbol in the box.

Location symbol

Continue straight for three squares.

Drive up one square.

Drive left one square.

Drive up three squares.

Destination: ____

Weather satellites are imaging and measuring instruments to track the weather on Earth.

Sputnik I was the first satellite. It sent back information about the temperature and pressure in Earth's atmosphere.

Communications satellites help send phone calls, radio and TV shows, and computer data.

The Global Positioning System, or GPS, uses satellites to pinpoint locations on Earth.

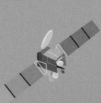

Have a go at drawing your own satellite. Look at the top image, then use the grid below to copy the picture square by square.

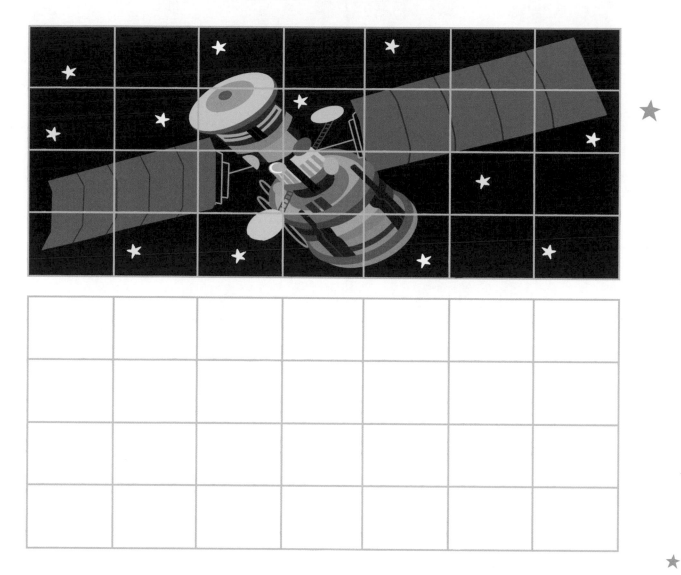

The military use powerful cameras and radio equipment on "spy satellites" to keep track of enemies.

Use the code cracker below to decode the secret message.

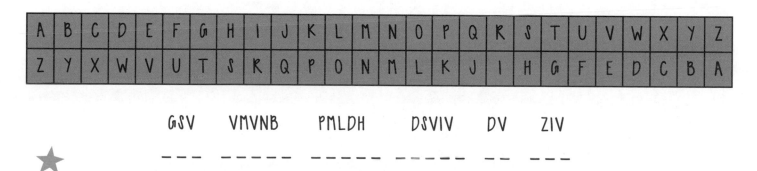

A	B	C	D	E	F	G	H	I	J	K	L	M	N	O	P	Q	R	S	T	U	V	W	X	Y	Z
Z	Y	X	W	V	U	T	S	R	Q	P	O	N	M	L	K	J	I	H	G	F	E	D	C	B	A

GSV   VMVNB   PMLDH   DSVIV   DV   ZIV

_ _ _   _ _ _ _ _   _ _ _ _ _   _ _ _ _ _   _ _   _ _ _

Scientists track space junk using telescopes and radar, to avoid collisions.

SPACE JUNK

There are millions of pieces of "space junk" floating around our planet. This includes old satellites, broken equipment, and rocket parts. Even flecks of paint can damage working satellites and spacecraft.

Take a look at the pieces of space junk below. How many of each can you find in orbit?

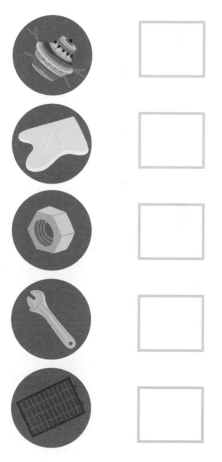

- Some pieces of space junk fall to Earth and are burnt up in the atmosphere. Sometimes junk is blasted farther away into space.

BEYOND THE SOLAR SYSTEM

The Universe contains at least 200 billion galaxies. Our home galaxy is the Milky Way. Our Solar System is just a speck within the Milky Way, and Earth is just a speck within the Solar System!

THE MILKY WAY

A galaxy is a huge collection of stars, gas, and dust, held together by the force of gravity. Galaxies can contain billions of stars. The Milky Way is our home galaxy.

Look at these different types of galaxies, then read the facts below to figure out which is which.

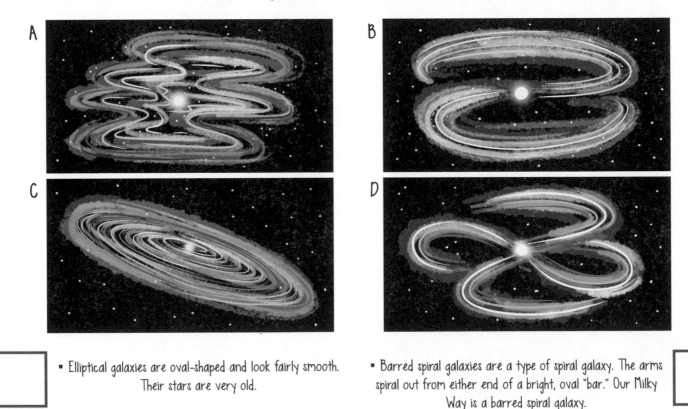

- Elliptical galaxies are oval-shaped and look fairly smooth. Their stars are very old.

- Barred spiral galaxies are a type of spiral galaxy. The arms spiral out from either end of a bright, oval "bar." Our Milky Way is a barred spiral galaxy.

- Spiral galaxies have curved arms that spiral out from a bright ball of stars in the middle.

- Irregular galaxies are shapeless blobs of gas and dust. They contain new stars.

Try using chalks to complete this picture sudoku. Each galaxy must only appear once in each row, column, and minigrid.

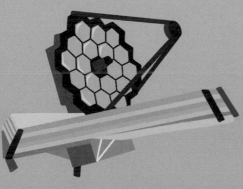

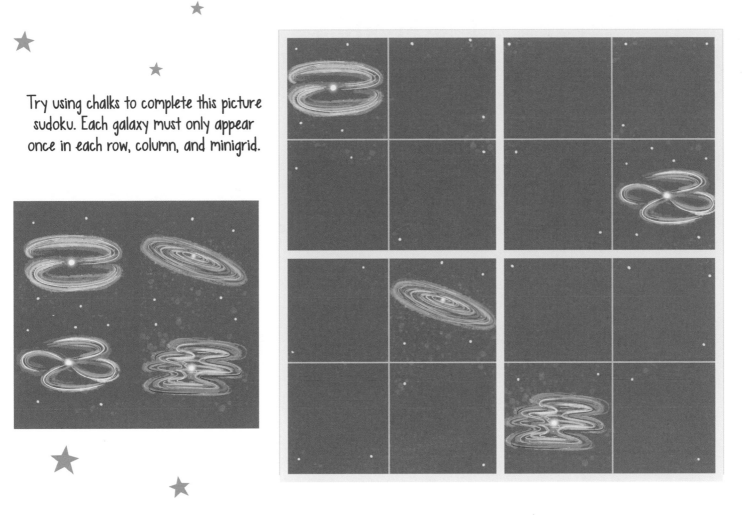

The James Webb Space Telescope (JWST) is the largest and most powerful telescope in space. The JWST is beaming back images of distant galaxies way beyond our Solar System.

Can you match the JWST to its silhouette?

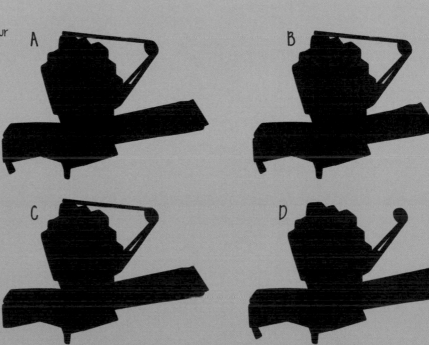

A

B

C

D

CONSTELLATIONS

If we look at the night sky, groups of stars form patterns, called constellations. There are 88 constellations, which are named after objects, animals, or characters from ancient myths.

Constellations are like dot-to-dot pictures in the sky. Join the dots on these constellations to reveal the pattern of each constellation.

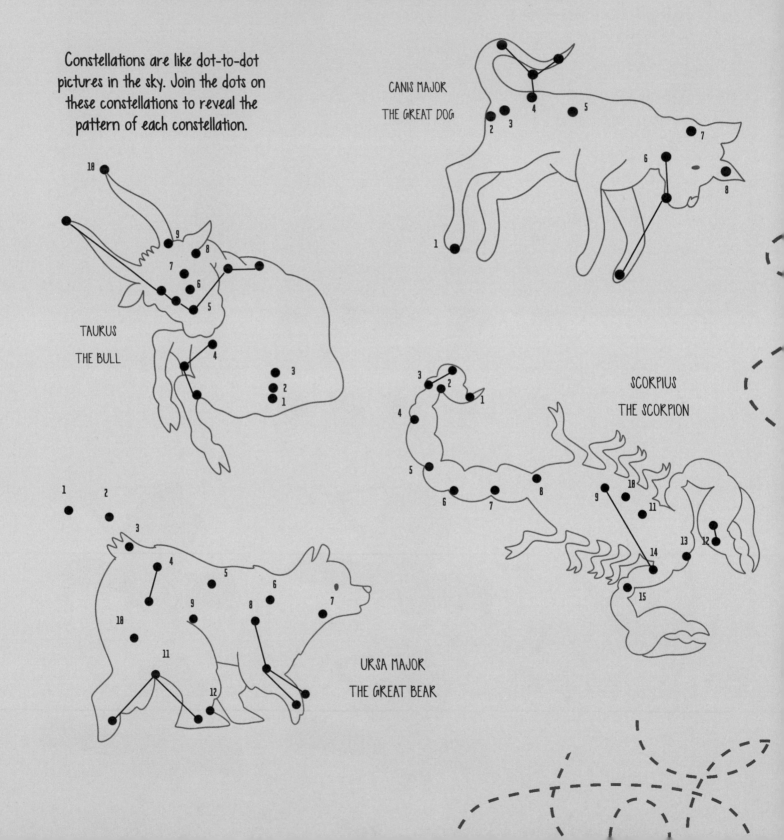

CANIS MAJOR

THE GREAT DOG

TAURUS

THE BULL

SCORPIUS

THE SCORPION

URSA MAJOR

THE GREAT BEAR

Orion is one of the most eye-catching constellations. Orion was a hunter in Greek mythology. Can you spot five differences between the two pictures?

- Within Orion's sword is the Orion Nebula. When seen through a telescope, it is a beautiful bright cloud of gas and dust.

- The bottom star on the right is called Rigel. It is the brightest star in Orion.

THE LIFE OF STARS

All stars go through different stages. They are born, they burn their fuel, and then, when their fuel runs out, they die.

A new star is born in a huge cloud of gas and dust called a nebula. Can you complete the jigsaw of the Eagle Nebula? Which piece doesn't fit?

A

B

C

D

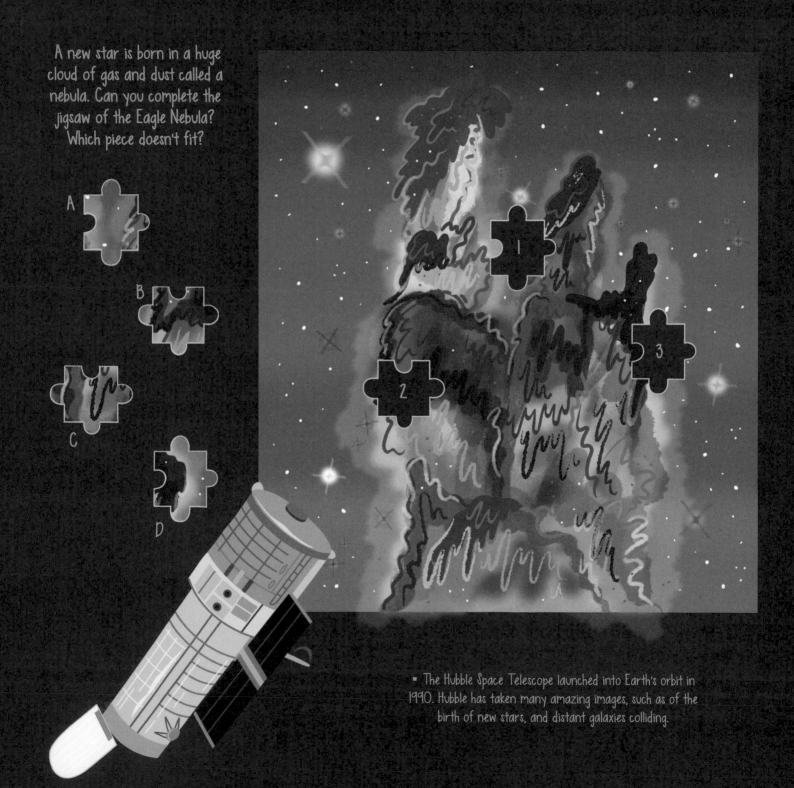

▪ The Hubble Space Telescope launched into Earth's orbit in 1990. Hubble has taken many amazing images, such as of the birth of new stars, and distant galaxies colliding.

Stars look different depending on their weight, and stage in their life cycle. Blue stars are the hottest and brightest. Red stars are cooler.

Read the facts, then use your brightest pens to fill in the stars.

1. Supergiant stars can be red or blue. They emit many times more energy than the Sun.

2. The Sun is an average-sized yellow star.

3. Blue giants are the brightest and hottest stars in the sky.

4. Red giants are average stars that are running out of energy. They can swell up to a size much bigger than the Sun.

1

2

3

4

Dwarf stars are old stars that are much smaller than our Sun. Most stars in our galaxy are red dwarfs. White dwarfs are even smaller and older. Count the red dwarf stars. Can you spot the white dwarf?

BLACK HOLES

There are areas in space with such immense gravity they swallow up everything that comes close—even light. These are black holes. Black holes can form when a supergiant star dies in a huge explosion called a supernova.

Some black holes can be a few times the size of the Sun, others are the size of entire galaxies. Put these black holes in size order, with 1 being the largest.

1. _____
2. _____
3. _____
4. _____
5. _____
6. _____

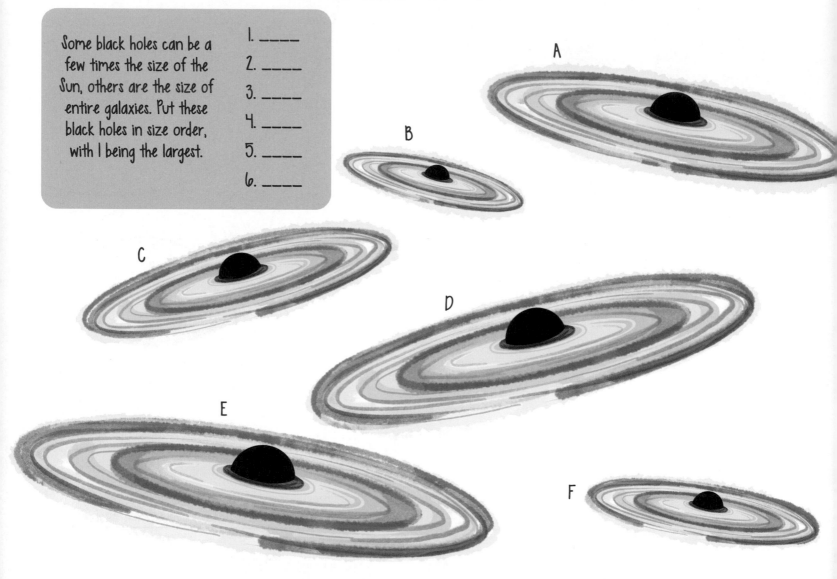

Any object that comes close is stretched into a long spaghetti shape by the black hole's extreme gravity, before disappearing completely.

Cross out all the letters X, Y, and Z to discover what this process is called:

XSYZPAZZGYHEXTZTIFYIZCAXYTZIOXNY

_____

Make your way through the space maze, avoiding the black holes as you go.
Beware of the supermassive black hole in the middle.

START

FINISH

▪ Scientists think there is a supermassive black hole in the middle of our galaxy, the Milky Way. Luckily, we are too far away to be sucked into it!

▪ Although black holes are invisible, scientists know they are there because bright swirling circles of matter form around them.

QUIZ

Now your voyage around the Solar System has come to an end, let's see how much you have learned. Have a go at this quiz and test your knowledge. The answers are on page 96.

1. What type of star is the Sun?

a) Orange giant

b) Yellow dwarf

2. What causes the aurora borealis?

a) The solar wind

b) Moonlight

3. Which is the smallest planet in the Solar System?

a) Mercury

b) Pluto

4. Which planet is known as the Red Planet?

a) Earth

b) Mars

5. What is the name of Jupiter's largest moon?

a) Ganymede

b) Phobos

6. Which planet is the windiest in the Solar System?

a) Uranus

b) Neptune

7. What is a meteoroid called when it lands on Earth?

a) Meteorite

b) Comet

8. What year did people first walk on the Moon?

a) 1969

b) 1972

9. What is the largest and most powerful space telescope?

a) James Webb Space Telescope

b) Hubble Space Telescope

10. What is the name of our home galaxy?

a) The Eagle Nebula

b) The Milky Way

ANSWERS

PAGES 4–5:

The eight planets are Mercury, Venus, Earth, Mars, Jupiter, Saturn, Uranus, and Neptune.

PAGE 6:
1. E
2. A
3. C
4. B
5. D

PAGE 7:
A. JUPITER 5
B. NEPTUNE 8
C. MARS 4
D. SATURN 6
E. EARTH 3
F. URANUS 7
G. VENUS 2
H. MERCURY 1

PAGE 8:
YELLOW DWARF

PAGE 9:

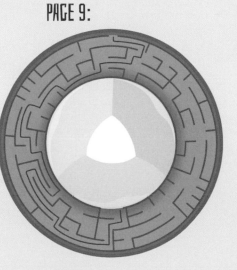

PAGE 10:
Mercury: 59 Earth days

Neptune: 16 hours

Jupiter: 10 hours

Venus: 243 Earth days

Jupiter has the shortest day.

PAGE 11:

A. Neptune. One year on Neptune is the equivalent of 165 Earth years!

1. b

3. c

4. a

5. d

Mars (2) doesn't have a silhouette.

PAGE 12:

There are 17 bubbles.

2 is the odd Sun out.

PAGE 13:

A2

B1

B3

C3

PAGE 14:

A. 1

B. 4

C. 3

D. 5

Jigsaw piece 2 doesn't fit.

PAGE 15:

I = A; 2 = B

Oxygen creates mostly green lights. Nitrogen creates blue, purple, and pink lights.

Saturn and Jupiter.

PAGE 16:

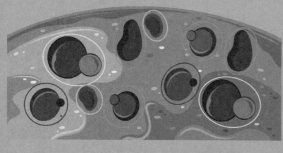

PAGE 18:

C. -180 °C (-290 °F).

IRON

PAGE 19:

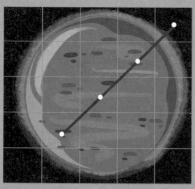

The Spider

PAGE 20:

There are 14 lightning bolts.

ROTTEN EGGS

PAGE 21:

1.

2.

3.

PAGE 22:

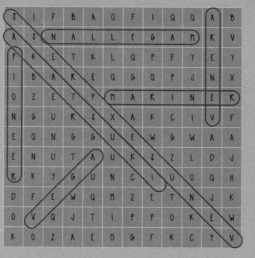

PAGE 23:

1, 8, 3, 6, 5, 4, 7, 2, 9.

PAGE 24:

PAGE 25:

E is the odd one out.

1. False. Earth is the third planet from the Sun.

2. True.

3. True.

4. False. Oxygen makes up about 21% of the atmosphere. Nitrogen is about 78%, and a mixture of other gases, including carbon dioxide, make up the remainder.

PAGES 26–27:

2 Crabs

3 Butterflies

7 Birds

5 Trees

8 Flowers

PAGE 28:

1. B
2. F
3. E
4. A
5. C
6. D

PAGE 29:

Carbon dioxide

PAGE 30:

Olympus Mons is nearly 3 times higher than Mount Everest.

True. It takes Mars nearly 687 days to orbit the Sun.

PAGE 31:

There is one Deimos left over.

PAGE 32:

PAGE 34:

1. Six
2. Oxygen
3. Rocks and soil
4. Jezero crater
5. Ingenuity

B

PAGE 35:

A and D

12

PAGE 36:

D

PAGE 37:

10

PAGES 38–39:

17

A. Europa

B. Io

C. Ganymede

D. Callisto

PAGE 40:

TITAN

1. False. Galileo discovered Saturn's rings more than 400 years ago.

2. False. Spacecraft cannot land on gas giant planets, as they do not have a solid surface.

3. True.

4. False. Titan is the second largest moon. It is just 2% smaller than Ganymede.

5. True.

PAGE 41:

PAGE 42:

A. 1

B. 2

C. 4

Jigsaw piece 3 doesn't fit.

Saturn has 7 rings.

PAGE 43:

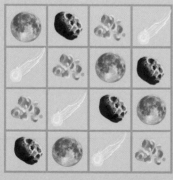

D

PAGE 44:

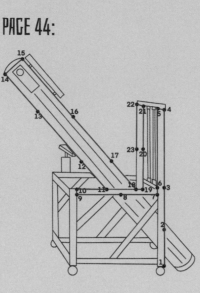

WILLIAM SHAKESPEARE

PAGE 45:

Uranus' rings were discovered in 1977.

PAGE 46:

There are 11 pictures of Uranus in the jumble.

Venus.

PAGE 47:

C

PAGE 48:

2

A

PAGE 49:

GREAT DARK SPOT

2. It takes Neptune 165 years to go once around the sun.

PAGE 51:

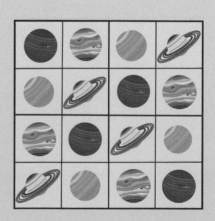

PAGE 52:

A. 5

B. 1

C. 6

D. 3

Pieces 2 and 4 do not belong.

PAGE 53:

B	D	U	B	C	S	T	I	D	C
E	A	C	F	D	E	G	E	R	O
F	H	S	I	G	I	C	E	H	J
K	M	E	T	E	O	R	O	I	D
I	L	J	C	E	K	K	M	K	L
N	M	R	O	N	R	E	O	T	P
P	Q	O	R	A	F	O	Y	S	E
H	S	C	O	Y	E	S	I	U	T
U	M	K	E	V	T	E	O	D	W
X	O	I	Y	D	D	Z	U	S	A

The dwarf planet's name is Ceres.

PAGE 54:

1. C-type

2. S-type

3. M-type

A	G	Y	A	K	P	A	N	D	N
I	K	D	M	A	Y	N	M	H	E
V	I	J	L	Z	X	U	Y	E	M
L	G	L	V	E	S	T	A	K	E
Y	A	W	K	K	Q	K	E	N	S
S	U	R	C	O	K	O	E	I	I
P	N	E	Q	N	I	F	B	O	S
D	N	M	K	U	U	P	D	N	A
P	E	M	B	J	S	H	Q	E	P
B	B	M	B	G	A	S	P	R	A

PAGE 55:

PAGE 56:

Meteoroids: 5

Meteors: 10

Meteorites: 3

PAGE 57:

D3

PAGE 58:

1. B

2. A

3. C

PAGE 59:

1. Eris

2. Makemake

3. Ceres

4. Haumea

PAGE 60:

C

PAGE 61:

There are 11 comets in total.

PAGE 62:

Jupiter: Io

Mars: Phobos

Saturn: Hyperion

Ida: Dactyl

Pluto: Charon

PAGE 64:

1. The Moon

2. 30

3. A boat

4. Because it reflects sunlight

5. 2

B

PAGE 65:

New Moon

Waxing Crescent

First Quarter

Waxing Gibbous

Full Moon

Waning Gibbous

Third Quarter

Waning Crescent

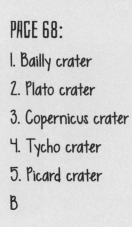

PAGE 66:

1. Blood moon

5, 3, 2, 4, 1

PAGE 67:

A and F

C and G

E and B

Glasses D do not have a matching pair.

PAGE 68:

1. Bailly crater

2. Plato crater

3. Copernicus crater

4. Tycho crater

5. Picard crater

B

PAGE 69:

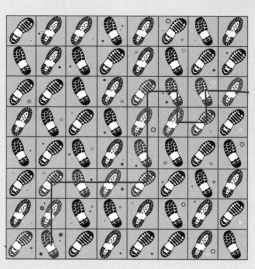

PAGE 70:

B

12 minutes

PAGE 71:

PAGE 72:

C. Dog

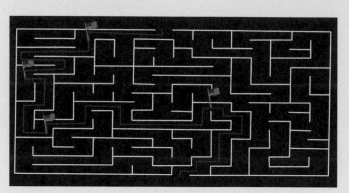

PAGE 73:

LRV location: E2

PAGE 74:

Maya exercised for the longest.

A and C

B and F

D and E

PAGE 75:

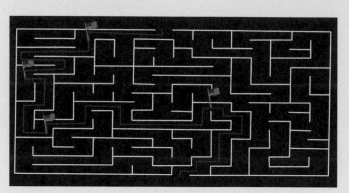

94

PAGE 76:

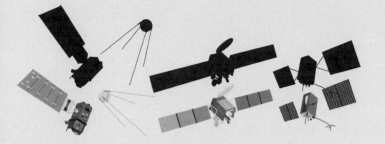

A. 4, B. 1, C. 3, D. 2.

C5

PAGE 77:

THE ENEMY KNOWS WHERE WE ARE

PAGES 78–79:

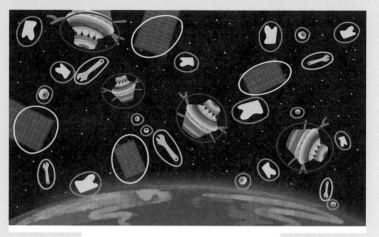

4   9   7   5   4

PAGE 80:

A. Irregular

B. Barred spiral

C. Elliptical

D. Spiral

PAGE 81:

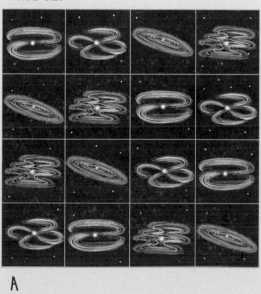

A

PAGE 82:

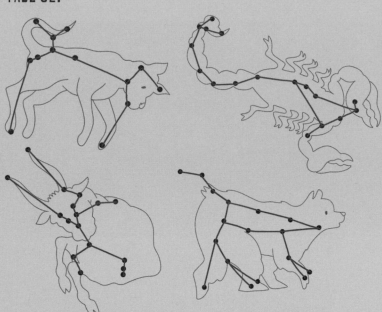

PAGE 83:

PAGE 84:

A. 1

B. 2

D. 3

Jigsaw piece C doesn't fit.

PAGE 85:

There are 13 red dwarf stars.

PAGE 86:

1. E

2. D

3. A

4. C

5. F

6. B

Spaghettification

PAGE 87:

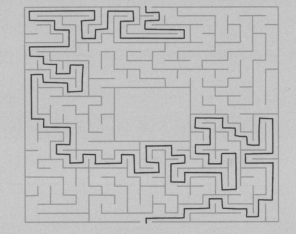

PAGE 88

1. b) Yellow dwarf

2. a) The solar wind

3. a) Mercury

4. b) Mars

5. a) Ganymede

6. b) Neptune

7. a) Meteorite

8. a) 1969

9. a) James Webb Space Telescope

10. b) The Milky Way